Becoming
ᴀWidow

An Anthology of Journeys
from Two to One

Kimbeth Wehrli Judge

Capucia LLC
211 Pauline Drive #513
York, PA 17402
www.capuciapublishing.com
Send questions to: support@capuciapublishing.com

Paperback ISBN: 978-1-954920-48-4
eBook ISBN: 978-1-954920-49-1
Library of Congress Control Number: 2022922226

Cover Design: Ranilo Cabo
Layout: Ranilo Cabo
Editor and Proofreader: Simon Whaley
Book Midwife: Carrie Jareed

Printed in the United States of America

Capucia LLC is proud to be a part of the Tree Neutral® program. Tree Neutral offsets the number of trees consumed in the production and printing of this book by taking proactive steps such as planting trees in direct proportion to the number of trees used to print books. To learn more about Tree Neutral, please visit treeneutral.com.

Dedication

In memory of the LoveStorm of my life,
honoring our significant efforts
to mature beyond our heritage.
And to our children, and theirs, and theirs,
as they further pursue the art of intelligent kindness

Contents

Introduction

I was widowed in June 2019, some twenty years after I inadvertently witnessed the suicide of a fellow contributor's husband. The story of how we two widows later came together and shared our grief experiences with other widows unfolds over the following chapters. Together, we learned that every woman's journey into widowhood is different, and we collectively took comfort in understanding each other's fears and concerns.

Most widows in this book claimed they were not writers. But we suggested they were, that they'd lived long and thoughtful lives, and that if they could describe them orally, they could put these thoughts onto paper. As further encouragement, we promised to edit their work and help them along the way. Every piece included here is wonderfully open and honest. Women possess a natural ability to be helpful, and so when these widows understood that their shared stories were purposeful, they all became the writer they said they weren't. That's the beauty—the catharsis gained through their writing experience, and the shared knowledge a reader may gain from all of us.

In my case, it's been over two years since being thrown into widowhood, and with that amount of time and writing behind me, I'm able to analyze my response to this new condition less dramatically, more levelheadedly, than in the beginning. What you'll notice as you read through these personal widowhood accounts is that although we ran the gamut of marital experiences, all of us managed to handle our husbands' deaths. And this is our collective key message: You can and will get through the grief and turmoil of circling back to becoming one again. You can choose to re-establish yourself as one, you can develop a pleasant routine, and become accustomed to yourself.

We women cope. We do it all our lives long, beginning with the semi-surprise and management of our monthly periods. Hands down, whether or not we bear children, we've got a monthly physical experience for a large part of our lives. So, yeah, we know how to cope.

The writers of this book know that widowhood affects us all differently, but with a commonality that begs sharing. Our lives are dramatically altered in ways both sad and disorienting. We've learned how to recover our true selves and live to write about it.

This book is dedicated to all of you as a reference, as a comparison, as a type of guide, and, most importantly, as comfort. We're here to embrace you. This may seem like a solitary journey, but you are not alone.

We originally intended to disclose the authors' names beside each firsthand story, as a way of proving our ode to honesty of thought. But, as it turned out, one author decided her story might somehow demean her dead husband's memory. Thoughtful dialogue could not dissuade her from either withdrawing from the project or presenting herself incognito.

I've concluded that her story is important and maybe even more so because of her caveat to protect her husband's honor. Part of me wished to do the same for my husband, a journalist who infamously laughed at the newsman's lament,

"Print the Legend." He had developed quite the public armor, and he was admired for his tough Chicago persona. Through my painfully honest exploration as his widow, I've chosen to skip the glorifying and apply his private behavior to the analysis of my struggle between loyalty and healing in our family story of me becoming his widow.

Kimbeth Wehrli Judge
(widowed three years)
Kimbeth writes for women. She spent her marriage of fifty-two years as a stay-at-home mother of three and wife of one, domestically focused on creating her imagined perfect family life, all the while writing about what she observed, taming her truth by calling it fiction.

She has published two books: a humorous collection of short stories called *Mothers And Others*, and a novel called *The FlipSide*.

Currently focused on this book, she's also writing a novel, which is much more fun. She continues the chore of restructuring her newly solitary self, balancing the isolation of writing by frequent gatherings with her loving and stimulating family and friends.

Me

Nancy Wehrli Pekarek

Widow, single mom, single person
Trying on new descriptors,
Like slipping into a new dress.
Tugging here, smoothing there;
Making it look good, finding a
Smile.

Fitting new onto same body
Like relining an old coat.
Will it ever feel "me?"
Can "me" overcome fading friendships? Find new ones?
Learn decision-making "oneness?"

Resisting, resenting, roiling in "oneness."
Feeling guilt; what could, should have been seen?
Transporting my mind to memories; many good, loving
And funny ones sustain "me."

Discovering uncharted paths; defining an "OK" day.
Wrapped in family love; someday "me" will browse for
A new pair of shoes.

**Nancy Wehrli Pekarek
(widowed fifteen years)**

Here's how she poetically describes her eighty-year-old self:

Midwestern, middle class
Large family, plenty of sass.

Higher education reached,
Graduate, then teach.

Raised four, then
Grandchildren galore.

Authored some books about them,
All in fun, nothing grim.

Now I put out my welcoming mat,
To my cozy Wisconsin flat.

Yesterday and Tomorrow

This is how I described my original encounter with widowhood, which is pretty much how I get a grip on where I am on any given day: what worked yesterday that might be useful for tomorrow...

Winter 2019

We'd driven to Florida for the fourth year running, to a wonderful rental on the beach that was ours for three months during Chicago's blustery February, March, and April.

Because we'd both gotten The Dreaded Flu the year before and cared for each other with the help of Zpacks pretty much throughout February, I located the best local Florida doctor the minute we arrived. She was booked solid for two months out, but we were glad to have nailed the appointment because Bernie "wasn't feeling great." He'd lost some weight, which appealed to him because his stomach was flatter, but he was strangely not hungry, and besides that, he wasn't sleeping well. I'd half-jokingly blamed it on his Irish attitude.

We often passed our time reading, and, ironically, one of my packed books was *Being Mortal: Medicine and What Matters in the End* (Atul Gawande, 2014). I'd so enjoyed the author's intelligently positive approach to life and death that I'd promised my book club I'd lead a discussion of it the following May. There it was for me to re-read, and so Bernie read it, too.

In it, Dr. Gawande suggests that instead of measuring life chronologically, we might be better served by measuring it experientially. He writes about palliative care: "dying with dignity"… the desire to go peacefully. Instead of lecturing, he includes personal stories about real people.

I didn't realize at the time how important these messages would become to the two of us.

Yet another irony besides the timing of our reading that book was that our lousy Florida television reception only clearly picked up *Jeopardy* at dinnertime. So that's what we enjoyed watching. One night, the host, Alex Trebek, announced he needed his audience to pray for him because he'd been diagnosed with pancreatic cancer. He told us to watch for the warning signs: sudden loss of weight, no appetite, sleeplessness. We stared at each other and uttered stunned phrases of, "Wow," "Yikes," "Christ," and "Good God," and then it was all about changing the subject. But really, the subject never did change after that, not in our minds, as we stoically inched toward our fate.

In late March, we met our doctor and liked her, and got the required blood work done.

Two days later, her nurse called Bernie to tell him his blood sugar count was 300 (ninety is the norm) and to come back for more tests. He did and was called back two days after that to be told that he had stage four pancreatic cancer that had spread to his liver.

Let's stop here for a moment because… WTF? Who arrives in Florida so under-cared for by their own Chicago physician that his blood health is that out of whack?

We packed up and drove home, unpacked, and went right on doing what was necessary. Bernie had choices of treatments to prolong his life, with painful therapies. He chose to live through his remaining weeks in our home with the pain management of cannabis and being lovingly surrounded by his children. (I've been asked how I felt about his end-of-life choices. My answer is this: As a couple, we were pragmatic under duress, and so I saw his directives as sensible and followed them smoothly. I did not question his need to die at home surrounded by me and our kids, because who was I to judge that call?)

My husband of fifty-two years, the father of our three children, and grandfather of their five, was dead in seventy-four days. Transitioning through a radical change this fast and this absolute is paralyzing.

I'm not a person who has the fallback of organized religion, nor do I personally value psychoanalysis, so I've decided to journal my way out of this... this life reduction.

Nine Months in and I'm Still Numb

I feel deserted. I feel abandoned and angry. I feel strangely free, but at the same time shackled to the past. My mood swings meet the standard of what I imagine bipolar disorder to be. I'm either euphoric about all that I'm accomplishing or forlorn about accomplishing so little.

I see myself as confused, functioning beautifully one day, and a paralyzed mess the next.

I've learned to recognize my good, productive days and fully use that energy to make up for the days I feel overwhelmed and unable to tackle the things I need to face and change.

There we were, living out the end part of a truly lively life together, not always great, but always together, occasionally stunning, and often pretty nice... and suddenly there's only one of us living out our life.

How does one do that?

Where's my workmate, my playmate, my sometimes source of annoyance and often pleasure?

I can see now, that in many ways, it will take me months and months of intense concentration to understand the complexity of losing a life partner who had, in all honesty, exhausted me into submission with his controlling ways. His ownership of me, once so appealing, had become a kind of incarceration, as we traveled through our later years together, with him having no hobbies other than me.

As much as I need to figure all of that out, I also need to own my end of the dance we'd danced, which had confused us both. Back in the sixties, with the naïveté of kids in their twenties and hotly in lust, we viewed our love as superior, saw the mess of other marriages, and knew we could do better. In many ways, we did: we remained pleasingly sexual and also able to amuse each other with conversation. He loved the way I mothered our children, and I vicariously loved his journalistic work life.

Things got trickier during the teenage years when undisciplined attitudes surfaced. Teenagers guiding teenagers!

My view of this is that Bernie and I had both experienced family traumas in our teenage years and therefore hadn't matured beyond that point in certain ways, certainly not enough to lead others gracefully through. I tried to be the grownup in the room. Bernie joined the kids in acting out, a pretty intense parenting *deal breaker* for me, which led to increased difficulties between us as a couple.

Through the years, as my husband stumbled with human interaction and rose in power, his need to be *fixed* (his amazingly candid words) and my determination to please him, dramatically intensified with me playing equal parts to his need of being his lover and his mother. (Quite the dance if you're simultaneously raising three innocents.)

Neither of us understood adult conflict resolution, and after what I'd witnessed as a child of divorce and coming from a war hero and an artist, all I knew was how to behave and look good.

He'd come from a household of alcohol and fury and had pretty much raised himself. He knew fighting and self-preservation. I knew defense and leadership, so we fought— and according to our kids, apparently more often and more dramatically than I choose to remember. All agree, we were lovely when we didn't.

Fifty-two years in, we'd all survived. The kids were formally educated and debt-free, married, and with kids of their own. And now wasn't this the part where you're worn out from the dance and grateful for the love that somehow got you through? Apparently not. Apparently, this was the part where, after all that, one of you leaves.

Six months after his death, an international plague plunged everyone on Earth into confused submission with disjointed information and unhinged political strife. I was, in some sense, already prepared because of my newly semi-isolated state of widowed existence.

Coronavirus feels far less radical to me than it does to some others. Even the COVID-19 daily death announcements are not as devastating to me, because my family so recently experienced the tragedy of losing our patriarch. So my reaction to all those deaths was empathy and gratitude. Unlike so many, at least our man had been surrounded by his dearest during his dying days.

Thinking It Through

Being a writer, I cope with life's traumas by writing my way into an understanding. I review the before and after, the lead-ups and consequences, what it all means to me, what my reaction could be, and then what it pragmatically should be. In this way, I settle myself down.

I get to solid ground.

After I began examining the trauma of my husband's death through writing, I found myself restlessly unable to conclude, to accept the stark reality, and to gracefully step into the forward unknown direction. I was alone for the first time in all of my seventy-five years.

I pondered this life-changing death endlessly, wondering if I wasn't actually better off alone, considering I'd remained an optimist and a physically healthy person. I began a hazy process of wondering how others coped.

Early on in my journey, I contacted a woman in my building with whom I'd wanted to speak frankly about using her tragedy as the beginning of my first novel. Years before, my husband and I had witnessed the suicide of her husband. This left me traumatized. I simply could not get it out of my mind. So finally, I wrote the description of that experience and realized it was a perfect set-up, a fantastically dramatic beginning for the mystery novel about survival I'd already started to work on.

And so it was that I imagined a life for this man, this neighbor I'd met, but did not know, as if it were a performance on stage. I created backstories for him and his imagined lover. Even though the story was far from his reality, I wanted to show the manuscript to his widow because of its tender nature. But, my husband, (as a world-weary journalist and company man) vehemently opposed my contacting her. Eventually, the novel was published without us ever connecting.

The act of not telling the widow had in fact bitten me right out of the gate during the first reading of my published book, held for my condo book club. Three of the twenty-two members chastised me for *using* their friend's tragedy. Stunned, I timidly argued that death by suicide was a human condition and did not belong to her, nor any one person. Still, though, I was internally crushed to think I'd upset her. Again, my husband advised me to let it go, that there could be legalities involved, and so on. Through our many years together, I learned that going against my husband was never to my advantage—or anyone's—so I sheepishly remained mum.

Six years later, I was a widow. I was on my own, grieving my aloneness, wandering through my fifty-two years of coupledom. I was sifting through our memories, some fantastic, many good and great, when my mind lit up on the sub-topic of marital disagreements and the sorting out of the many reactions I'd have handled differently had I been on my own all along.

It occurred to me that I could cleanse my soul. I could use the step nine technique of Alcoholics Anonymous wherein the alcoholic apologizes to anyone he/she has hurt, allowing the victim to respond in whatever way they need to put the matter at rest, to make amends.

Clearly, this connection seemed meant-to-be because, then widowed for some twenty years, the widow, Nancy, (having heard of my recently widowed condition through our condominium grapevine) invited me to her place to console me. As we were getting to know each other, we spoke about our careers. She mentioned her banking background, which led me to mention my writing. It turned out she didn't know I was an author, and she hadn't read my work. We were both fairly thrown by this. I shared my apparently misguided fears about using her husband's tragedy to open my novel about survival. Her reaction was curiosity, so later that night, I left the book by her door.

Several days later, she invited me back to her home and told me, tearfully, that this was the first accurate account of her husband's suicide she'd heard or read. She found it very painful. I was beyond remorseful at having re-opened her eyes, but she told me it was OK, that she understood, that she enjoyed my imagined plot and liked my writing style.

We sat awhile with our thoughts, mine filled with admiration for her generosity of spirit, hers stimulated by our newfound friendship. When she asked me what I was currently working on, I told her. "I'm pondering a work of non-fiction about what's involved in becoming a widow, to help me through the fresh trauma of it."

As we discussed my writing as my method of self-soothing, she warmed to the idea… and so began the slow movement toward her trying it out herself. Several weeks later, she handed me a succinctly written depiction of her twenty-year experience. We read our widowhood manuscripts aloud to each other and discussed the comparison of my one year of widowhood juxtaposed to her twenty, curious and pleased at the way the two play off of one another.

I described my latest vision of a helpful book, this one possibly including the contributions of others such as herself, and, out of all this, we somehow easily slid into becoming partners. We encouraged a couple of other widows to write their own chapters, to join our endeavor of creating a sort of self-help book, but more than that, a collection of courageously true accounts of legitimately traumatic journeys. Months later, Nancy and I hosted seven widow-reading luncheons.

Widowed by Suicide

Nancy Seever Hunter

On Sunday, June 1, 2003, I went to a Chicago Cubs game with three women friends. When I left, I knew my husband was upset. He had lost his job in the middle of May and was wondering what he would do with the rest of his life. We were financially comfortable, and I had a successful consulting business. My parting words to him were that we would figure it out together, and that I loved him. (I have often wondered how my life would be different if there had not been a baseball game that afternoon, but clearly, the *wondering changes nothing*.)

At the end of the seventh inning, I called Jack and asked him to take the hamburgers we were going to grill for dinner out of the refrigerator. I told him I would be home in approximately two hours and then said my last words to him, "Honey, I love you." I was in a good mood and looking forward to a relaxing evening.

It's an easy public transportation ride (L ride) from Wrigley Field to close to where I live in Chicago, and a short walk from the L stop to my condo building. As my friends and I approached my building, I knew something was wrong. Police and firemen were circling the building. The husband of one woman who had attended the game with me was waiting outside my building and told me Jack had committed suicide by throwing himself out of the window of our twenty-seventh-floor condo.

The police followed me upstairs and asked if there was any way they could help me. Neighbors were very kind and helpful. I was numb and a wreck.

Jack's family (sister, brother, and their children) who lived out of town had to be told and then, of course, the multitude of friends that we had accumulated through the years were notified. Jack's mom was still alive but in the serious stage of dementia. His sister and I decided it was best to leave Nan with her memories. My parents had died several years earlier. My only sibling, a sister, had died the previous year.

To say people were *shocked* is an understatement. For the next few days, there was lots of activity. People were in and out of my condo, bringing food, wanting to be sure I was OK, and, of course, offering their condolences. But I knew that eventually the activity would stop and I would be left alone to figure out the next stage of my life.

I was fifty-eight years old, had known Jack for over fifty years, and been married to him for twenty-six years. We were neighbors growing up. We had dated when I graduated from college and I had moved back home before deciding to get a place of my own in downtown Chicago. Jack wanted to move to Dallas and work for American Airlines for a while. We quit dating amicably and both went our own way for seven years. When we ran into each other one lunchtime, he asked me to join him at a nearby restaurant, The Italian Village, and we never stopped seeing each other after that. Two years later, we were married.

I was thirty-two when we married and Jack was thirty-three. I had a successful career, and so did Jack. Both of us kept a degree of independence while also sharing many interests.

Jack loved golf, I played a little. We loved to travel. We rehabbed two condos and built a house. I had huge respect for Jack's design skills and his sense of adventure. He was wonderful to my family. He would often stop by my dad's condo in Oak Brook just to say Hi. Simply put, I loved him and he was the kindest person I ever knew.

Most of all, I realize now how many wonderful people are in my life because of Jack… his sister and her husband, nieces and a nephew, and their children—a goddaughter and godson and the families they've created. He asked me to give up the city for a while and have an adventure in St. Charles, a suburb fifty miles west of Chicago. Because of the way he encouraged me to gather freely with my single women friends throughout our marriage, my friendships have expanded enormously. To this day, I consider several of those people among my dearest friends.

I loved the many people Jack and I got to know in the last place we lived together, the high-rise where his terrible tragedy happened, and where I still live. The list goes on and on, but let's go back to when the last guests leave your home.

You shut the door and you realize you are alone and must create a different life.

I got up on Monday, June 10, 2003, and went to work, experiencing, once again, a flood of attention. Getting started again, knowing that Jack would not be home when I finished work, left a pit in my stomach. In the evening, I drank gin and smoked cigars. After doing this for about two weeks, I finally admitted I really don't like gin and, except for a few weeks in college, never smoked. I wasn't hurting Jack. I was only hurting myself.

During the first year, I had to meet with attorneys and financial consultants. I had been named the executor of my dad's and sister's estates. Consequently, I knew what to expect, but when it is your husband and so unexpected, the pain is much more *intense* and also *lonely!*

I also had to decide if I wanted to stay in the condo we had rehabbed together. I loved where I lived. Good friends and a wonderful building staff—so respectful, helpful, and kind—convinced me I should not move too quickly. To this day, almost twenty years later, the staff and building friends that were so helpful hold a very special place in my heart.

Over time, there were many questions. What happened? Why? Was I OK? Did I need anything? There were even some inappropriate questions. Eventually, they subsided. I learned quickly it is OK to put boundaries on questions and worked on developing a response to questions I felt were inappropriate. I found, "Thank you for asking, but I am just not prepared to discuss it at this time," worked very well.

Of course, I kept thinking, *Is there something about Jack—a surprise—that I didn't know about?* Fortunately, however, my estate attorney recommended I probate the estate, which means that, after it is closed, no one can sue the estate for anything. There have been several times when someone "representing a law firm" called and said he was going to sue the estate if I didn't give him a lot of personal information. It is easy to get sucked into these scams. I was confident because I had followed my attorney's simple advice to hang up. The only *surprise* from Jack was a $50 speeding ticket.

I also realized that, over time, things would never be the same, but day-to-day living would return. People invited me to lunches and dinners. The neighbors on my floor asked if I would like to participate in a floor barbecue that became a special tradition for many years. Friends surprised me with a wonderful sixtieth out-of-town birthday weekend party. Long-established holiday traditions continued.

I also was familiar with the five stages of grief (denial, anger, bargaining, depression, and acceptance) that Elizabeth Kübler-Ross discussed in her book *On Death and Dying* (Simon and Schuster, 1969). Like so many others who have gone through tragedy and loss, I felt myself go in and out of the stages, and still do, even almost twenty years later.

A friend suggested I go into therapy, and I did for a short period of time. I found it helpful, but the therapist said I was not stuck. I had a picture of what I wanted my future to look like. She gave me *very good* final advice. She said, "When you feel like crying, just let it come. Don't put it off. If you are driving, pull over and cry. Just let it come." She suggested even years in the future, "Something may remind you of your loss and you will start crying again. That's normal and OK." She was right. On a beautiful fall day, I remember how many fun times we had going to The University of Wisconsin football games, or at Christmas when *Blue Christmas* comes on the radio, the tears always come. Every time I walk by The Italian Village I well up! Going by a golf course, watching an exciting match on TV, or revisiting places we traveled to brings back so many memories!

Several books also helped me during this difficult time. A dear friend's daughter sent me a copy of Sarah Ban Breathnach's *Simple Abundance: 365 Days to a Balanced and Joyful Life* (Grand Central Publishing, 1995). I found it was so helpful and encouraged me to focus on gratitude rather than anger. Erin McHugh's *One Good Deed A Day: 365 Days of Trying to Be Just a Little Bit Better* (Chronicle Books, 2012), and Julie Steines and Virginia Freyermuth's *Norbert's Little Lessons For A Big Life* (Gallery Books, 2017) are two books that are just fun, gave me a boost, and still do.

I continued working. New people came into my life. One special couple wanted to know if I wanted to go to

San Miguel, Mexico, with them on a trip sponsored by the Art Institute of Chicago. Although I was concerned about being *alone* and traveling with a couple, they were kind and gracious. I am so glad I accepted their invitation and their special friendship through the years.

Then, in 2005, I learned I had breast cancer. Again, my support group was there for me during this very difficult time. When I was given a clean bill of health, I made arrangements with my business partner to work part-time for the next eighteen months. At the end of that period, I was ready to retire and sold my interest in the business to him.

During my part-time status, I decided that when I fully retired, I'd spend six months in Europe. At first, I thought of Rome, but the same friends who included me on their trip to Mexico said they had a friend who had a condo in Paris that she wanted to rent. The condo was in the 16th arrondissement (district), near the Eiffel Tower—a perfect location! After looking at pictures and meeting with the owner, I decided the three-bedroom, three-bath, six-month rental was worth the price and started making plans. My roommate from college, Marianne, was divorced, had two grown sons, and was looking for a reason to retire from her long teaching career. I asked Marianne to join me for the six months and she readily agreed. On August 1, 2007, we headed off to Paris. It was a terrific experience! We met wonderful new people, had friends from the States visit us, traveled around Europe, and had one marvelous adventure after another. Leaving February 1, 2008, was not easy, but there were still things left to do back home.

I found re-entry more difficult than I had expected. I was coming up to the fifth anniversary of Jack's death. Buying a new car by myself was sad. I realized I could never share with Jack my Paris experience. Being completely retired and not having a place to go to in the morning left me a little at loose ends. I dated a little but found no one I wanted to spend more than dinner with. Time went by. In 2009, Marianne and I took an apartment in NYC for several months, but it was not nearly the fun of Paris. I continued to travel internationally with my single women friends and have been on seven continents with an Australian widow I met in Canada in the fall of 2003.

One afternoon, I was sitting in my living room looking out over Grant Park and Lake Michigan, and I decided to join WW (WeightWatchers). I had put on weight during the years and made a commitment to take it off. It turned out to be a terrific decision. I looked forward to the weekly meetings and the camaraderie of the group. Most of all, I liked having a goal and the encouragement everyone gave me. From my heaviest, I lost sixty pounds and just felt better about myself. The success made me feel like reaching out to people again.

If you are open to them, living in a big city affords many fun learning experiences. I decided to take advantage of those opportunities. There are all kinds of lectures to attend. After a while, I began to make new friends (friends who didn't know Jack but who were interested in the things I find enjoyable). I became a member of The University Club of Chicago, the Art Institute of Chicago, the Chicago Architecture Foundation, and The Chicago Council on Global Affairs, to name a few. Again, these memberships opened new people and experiences to me.

Recently, I have taken an interest in jazz and expect to be going to several concerts when indoor events start opening after the pandemic.

Jack's family continues to be close. Before COVID-19 I saw them regularly. Several years ago, his grandniece spent a summer at an internship in Chicago and lived with me for three months. It has also been a joy to me to see our godchildren and their families grow and prosper. I continue to love and appreciate the many memories of people who have been so supportive.

Do I still miss Jack? *You Bet!!!* I see my friends and their husbands getting older and I wonder, what would we have been like? I miss the bantering that goes on with a married couple. That can be irritating, but so often leads to better decisions. I miss his energy, sense of humor, his enthusiasm. I just miss him.

However, I also realize I am very fortunate that I loved him and had him in my life as long as I did. My goddaughter said that you can play marriage like a tennis match: you can be in a singles match lobbing the ball back and forth, or you can join forces and be a very powerful team playing a doubles match. I like to think Jack and I were at our best when we played the doubles match.

No matter how much I still miss Jack, I am happy. It is a different kind of happiness, but I have been able to make new friends, have different experiences, and laugh.

Before I end, I feel I would be remiss if I didn't say a few final remarks about suicide. Since Jack's death, I have learned the magnitude of people who are affected by this horrible disease. Family, friends, acquaintances, and even strangers have approached me when they learn I am a suicide widow, wanting to be comforting and also to be comforted about suicide experiences they had with spouses, children, other family members, or friends! I don't have any easy answers. I simply say, "Mental illness is a terrible disease. It is nothing you said or did." I ask if I can hug them. Sometimes I ask to be hugged. I try to be honest and encouraging.

I did not choose to join a support group, but I know people who have and I would strongly encourage those who feel they would benefit from one, to do the research and find one that fits their needs.

Mental illness is nothing to be ashamed of. It is a medical condition, just like heart disease or diabetes. As a society, we often struggle to understand the condition and to be of help. We need further understanding and guidance to approach this condition intelligently and someday eradicate the disease.

Please keep us in your prayers.

Nancy Seever Hunter
(widowed nineteen years)
Nancy and her husband, Jack, were close friends in childhood and, because they experienced their college educations and independent adult lives separately throughout their twenties, they were able to appreciate and encourage each other's independence when they re-united and married in their early thirties.

Nancy happily continued her banking career for thirty years and then used that knowledge to establish a small human resources consulting firm. And Jack happily continued his entrepreneurial endeavors and his golfing and piloting pastimes. Without the responsibility of children, they freely explored their country and traveled the world together.

Like everyone else, she experienced the COVID-19 virus curtailing much of her freedom. That said, she intends to continue exploring the seven continents in the company of her many friends and loving family.

Digesting My Truth

Twenty Months In, I Feel Better.

Although I would not have chosen to lose my married life of yesterdays and enter into unfamiliar tomorrows, here I am. I have developed a routine balanced with pleasant anticipation. I know myself better than ever before.

The people in my life, the ones I truly love and trust, are basically my immediate family, plus a few relatives and friends. There's no question that the calls and visits from my children and grandchildren nourish my need to give and receive love. I would not have picked myself up so quickly if it hadn't been for the example of strength I was compelled to put forth for the children's sake (my kids and theirs). Suddenly, all was completely up to me—The Matriarch. True, I no longer had to weather my husband's aggression interfering with the family calm, but the kids and grandkids missed his manly love for them—I did too.

In the end, I found that graceful living boils down to self-discipline. After tiring myself out with the escape of too much television and too much sleep, I craved stability. No more endless television, filled with the discomfort of babbling judgmental talking faces. Television was relegated to the nightly news. Newspaper reading was reduced from three to one, and only over breakfast. Three meals a day, the healthy kind I'd provided my family for all those yesterdays, was reinstated for the only one still home—Me. I'd paid attention to myself in a more useful way than maybe ever before, and through these many months, I'd come to realize that I was able to create a happy existence for myself. I'd learned that I need to stay busy, to have a purpose, to focus on chosen activities—my writing, my book clubs, my safely chosen people with informed opinions and positive attitudes.

The way that the love of my life announced his courageous decision burns in my memory. It was the day we'd seen his Chicago doctor, who had explained Bernie's charts and described the options for lengthening his life, possibly a year filled with sporadically intense pain. Then his doctor left us to decide, silently facing each other in that small sterile room with the papered examination slab and blinking computer. I waited for Bernie to say what we both knew to be true. He'd stared at me with such tender sadness and, after a while, he said, "I think I'm going to have to just die." My heart slows every time I think of it.

Bernie remained controlling to the end, but this time, his motives were all about protecting those precious few he loved. When he understood his fate, he used his limited energy to wrap things up efficiently. He astonished us all by allowing our knowledgeable daughter to treat his pain with cannabis. With our younger daughter, he lovingly accepted the concept of her Reiki skills and calmly submitted to her treatments. He called a home meeting with our investment advisors and our son, arranging seamless transfers of ownership to ensure my financial independence. Another home meeting was called to plan his funeral with our son's priest, assuring that our eldest daughter's Jewish faith be ceremoniously validated as well. He called for our grandchildren to visit, to say goodbye, to avoid their potential sadness if he died without them hugging him one last time. He requested that our three children spend the last remaining days and nights of his life camping out at our home together. In other words, at his insistence, we were all in this together.

As fate would have it, we had just established home care when a stroke left him unable to speak or walk. He could see and he could smile and he could frown. He could speak gibberish which, interestingly, only our son could understand. This male bonding connection was hugely helpful during our remaining time together.

Little did we know what a disastrously chaotic experience it would become. We were about to discover that the home care industry, at least at that time in Chicago, was abysmally run and that we'd all need to become protective watchdogs. I ordered him a hospital bed to be placed in the living room. The nurses were stationed at the large dining room table beyond his bed. They came and went, randomly replaced by others who often complained about the mess left by the last one. Our three kids settled in to sleep in the guest bed and on our couches. We warriors monitored the inadequate staff, checking their lists, and timing his needs.

We coexisted as a team on our assigned mission, warriors, yes, but so much more because of our need to love his soul firmly and gently out of his human body and into the relief beyond. We amused him with favorite family memories (he was the star of most as the bewilderingly stern father figure). He spent his last couple of weeks bedridden, able to hear the chatter of his family lovingly talking about him and earnestly planning his farewell country club luncheon to be held after the church service. (This, by the way, was an interesting revelation because he hadn't, in earnest, been to church for sixty years, and we had long ago denounced private clubs as exclusionary.) Scattered in our own religious beliefs, we four understood through literature that this is a typical end-of-life response, and so we simply carried out his wishes.

We managed all of this despite dealing with the agency difficulties of summer staffing shortages resulting in several shifts of non-English-speaking nurses, and—all the while—grieving for our dying man, a man so tough that most had expected him to outlast us all. His determination to stage us in this way had the effect of bonding us as never before. We snarkily nicknamed ourselves "The Fabulous Four."

Tomorrow arrived on June 14, 2019. He just stopped breathing, and that was it. We were required to continue, and he wasn't.

Much further down the road and halfway into creating this book, I experienced a personal reality check. After months of working with my widows, editing their copy, agreeably insisting on the integrity of their work and their total honesty (because without that, what's the point of any kind of sincere advice?), I realized that my own story lacked full disclosure.

I now see how thoroughly those dark years before my husband's death affected me. People were concerned because I did not cry over his death. Two years later, I still have not. When asked directly, I'd close it off by saying I didn't know why.

But I think I do.

I took my husband's death personally, as a reckless act of selfish disregard because he chose to self-soothe with alcohol, thus nursing his inner turmoil, which not only harmed him but also negatively affected me and our kids. The effort it took to withstand his life rage and self-medication through alcohol had left me exhausted. So no, I haven't cried these last couple of years.

A half-century ago, he asked me to save him from his dark side (his words). I tried. For our entire time together, I tried to shift his attitude from negative to positive, from the dark rage at what isn't to the sunny appreciation for what is. Although I see now that this was an impossible request—still, I'm left with the knowledge that I spent much of my life struggling to complete that challenge.

I not only couldn't shift his dark attitude, but I failed to complete myself, hoping for a rosier outcome by humoring him, and by drinking with him. Even as we aged, we did not reach serenity together. His brain power and his love for me got him halfway there. He split his attitudes and became a sort of public poser, but even then, he left quite a path of off-balance fans in his wake, all of us becoming ever more skilled at spontaneous reactions.

That's a lot, and I'm not complaining. Actually, I'm guessing there are plenty of similar stories out there. But here's the thing: all that effort, and still he's gone, leaving me to, finally, care for myself. With not that much time left, I'm hardly going to use it up with a pity party.

I miss the hopefulness of youth, the "anything is possible" beginning of our love story. I miss the younger, buoyant Bernie, the charismatic whip-smart man who'd somehow positioned himself into an amazing place of journalistic leadership and power. We absolutely had some glorious years together in our pleasant American bubble of time—back before the internet exploded the slow-moving structure of middle-class American security, confusing truth with harmful gossip and leading to fabricated fact. The learning curve of instant messaging was drastically misunderstood.

So, in my opinion, is the learning curve of successful aging. As *war babies*, my husband and I took our comfortable lives in stride. We surely did not see our struggle toward the end coming down the road.

American culture seems to encourage the misconception that retirement is a playful time to look forward to. While there's lots to be said for enjoying the high, the same could be said for planning ahead. My life circumstances were such that I never stopped re-adjusting. Turns out that's a key to life. Here I am, an old widow, and I don't see my position as negative. I see it as a curiosity, powered up with a lifetime of solid knowledge to guide me forward.

The end of us was sad. There's probably no way around that part. Choice-less in my eventual realities as the protective one in charge of Bernie's slow walk to death, I began arranging a few solid family memories: a professional family photograph was taken as a permanent record of his charm and health. To keep his spirits up, I executed extra gatherings meant to serve as happy anticipations for him, which they did, but he was often too weak to remain at those events.

My goal was to live it out quietly together, pretty much however he wanted—within reason. I refused to be his *anger enabler*. My honing of the tough and tender approach became even more significant as he seamlessly slipped in and out of rage. I learned to differentiate between his unacceptable angry lashing out at me (the only one there), and his need to vent with someone (me again, but what's a mother for…)

In truth, this kind of slow ride to widowhood is a sadly solitary existence, but, hands down, the only lovingly pragmatic way to go through those years is to be patient. I share this with you, my readers, as a comfort. To be evermore direct about what life is truly like ends up as a type of universal relief, which is nothing I'd ever share with a child because what a killjoy to know about life's deterioration. Yet, I have found pleasure in homeschooling myself, and, in that way, even familiarizing myself with this current newly widowed period in my seventy-eight years has been educationally fascinating.

Past Facts and Future Movement

I am safely secured alone in a condominium that I own and can afford to maintain, and I'm able to visit my kids, grandkids, and friends. If I want to, I can develop new friendships, I can travel, and I can stay awake for two days writing and not change clothes. And I can have ice cream for dinner, although it's best to have a salad first.

Statistically, most of us women have, or will become, widows because we seem to live healthier and longer, and arguably more determinedly. If I'd thought this through before it was upon me, I may have behaved differently earlier on. I have learned to embrace my sudden aloneness as a new beginning, a chance to live more intentionally beneficial to me—just me—because now that I'm getting used to it, it's not all bad. As time passes, I breathe better, easier than ever before.

After Two Solid Years, a Moment of Fatigue

Let's recognize the negative here, for just a moment or two. There seems to be some creepy backward movement happening exactly during my personal need to plunge forward. Beginning with Bernie's seventy-four-day-death-march, negative change has seemingly gripped the world stage.

Backward movement is beyond depressing. It's deflating and debilitating in a hopeless kind of way. And yes, I get to take a bow here. I have a legitimate claim to the double whammy of even greater pain as a person having already experienced the end of a fifty-two-year union, and on my way to god knows what, slogging through who knows how long this widowed existence will continue. This is because while I'm actually at the acceptable age of gracefully dying (in my sleep, please), my parents lived into their eighties and my maternal grandmother lived into her late nineties, and her mother went on into her hundreds (shoot me, please…). Here's my point: With my relevancy seemingly in shadow, I now have a *who cares* attitude, because, yes, my children and grandchildren give me great joy, but my own position and my larger world feel so disintegrating.

Wandering in the negative unknown is never a good idea, so I'll close it off with this: Please God, make this current existence be the dress rehearsal that is notoriously messy, and let us perform professionally for our packed audience on the real opening night. Can we all just wake up from this nightmare of consequences? Can the real show be the beautiful one for which we've rehearsed and rehearsed and rehearsed and rehearsed? Have we really missed the mark of worldwide good leadership that badly? Can we humans truly not follow the one Golden Rule?

August 2021 Has Arrived

I've now lived through a two-year downward spiral, which has left me in a fairly joyless state. I've purposely concentrated on my late husband's faults, an obvious ploy to stop missing him so dramatically, but a spade is a spade. Truthfully, I can no longer distinguish between missing him and simply missing the younger life we experienced together.

The almost constant talk around people my age is about America's poor leadership. Since the end of World War Two, we can be faulted for bringing our country to its knees through negligence, through not facing mistakes, through behaving egotistically and greedily. We seem to believe that we are a damaged country whose leaders have ignored its physical and mental stability. We need to repair our crumbling infrastructure and stop misusing our natural resources. We need to establish educational equality for all our citizens. Unenlightened, uncared-for people will forever prevent us from reaching our potential for goodness, for healthy forward development. Period.

America was facing its day of reckoning even before the pandemic, even before nature finally took its revenge over human lack of respect and threw fires and flooding and drought at us. And wind. Let's not underestimate the brutality of the wind. The new type of propaganda came in the form of misinformation, and bald-faced lying served up by the politicians and easily moved along by Big Money controlling the press.

My husband was an ethical journalist in America's news gathering heyday of practical honesty. Observing the deliverance of public information move from reporting factual truths to presenting unchecked sensationalism, and the move from integrity to greed fed his rage. This encouraged his drinking, which took its toll on his mind and body health.

So how am I keeping myself positive during this time of what I see as a national illness, newly combined with my widowed grief? Not smoothly. Not in a way that could help anyone else. Not certainly as an adviser. I've become far less confident about this book's importance. Not one of us widows can say they don't miss their mates every day. Every. Day.

We Chicagoans still have a violence epidemic, a disrespected police force, an educational crisis, a hungry underclass, and we world-weary survivors of misguided COVID-19 health welfare are still confused about a clear path out of this.

There isn't one.

We're currently experiencing a pivotal moment with no solid future plan in place. *But.* If we use this monumental mess we're facing to assess the facts honestly, this horrendous moment in time could actually become significantly positive.

I do not consider strengthening my husband and raising our children to have been *at my expense*, because I managed the supposed sacrifice of personal freedom well enough to use it constructively. I've grown into a person who understands the life of a middle-class American stay-at-home wife and mother, *and* I can write about it. It wasn't an easy road.

There isn't one.

The journey is the adventure and, apparently, I've got another one—this one—without my life partner, heartbreakingly sad, but still with not many dull moments because of our children and theirs.

By the time my husband died, we'd completed his vision of aging in his two chosen places, based upon his mental and physical security. We lived nine months in the heart of Chicago, the city he knew inside and out, where he'd experienced enormous personal success. And we lived three months in the dreamy climate comfort of a Florida beach home, where he could relax and recall his glory days, happily hosting our grown children and their children.

That was his, his vision. Now that his taps have played… RIP and so on, I need to figure out my vision, and this I think will take a while because…

There isn't one.

My Ultimate Reconciliation

There's a wall in my kitchen filled with framed photos of my late husband, playing off a large portrait done by an artist nasty enough to recognize the belligerent side of my husband and capture it perfectly. I actually hadn't noticed the effect it was having on me until a smothering stage of overall dissatisfaction began consuming my thoughts, not quite getting the oxygen needed for each breath.

This morning, I arose after fitful sleeping and found myself clearing that wall with a kind of excited relief. How had it taken so long to rid myself of that discomfort? Two and a half years!

This activity seems to be in pursuit of my supposed Act Three. The way I've got it figured out, only one of us was going to carry on, and apparently I was better equipped. *If* that's true (plenty of room for debate) then here I go, clearing my vision of such conflicts as the painted depiction of my belligerent drinker husband—*no longer* staring at me in my kitchen, and freeing my mind to enjoy the many pleasant photographs throughout my home of his happy, positive times.

Whether or not you're of my opinion, that life is a grand experiment, doesn't matter. It becomes moot after reading and listening to enough accounts of human behavior. I can, for example, generalize that we all basically learn by living, that we evolve slowly over time spent in certain daily routines—working, waking, sleeping, peeing, cooking, eating, crapping, listening, learning, speaking, giving, taking, helping, hindering, loving, hating, watching, judging—all the while, more or less, maintaining where and how our days are done. Then we die. Or, arguably, almost worse, someone we love dies. What was that all about? And if we're *old*, the loss seems confusing. Our daily performance is down to one. But if we don't pick ourselves up and realize some purpose, what then?

The days need filling.

January 6, 2022, 11:00 p.m.
I'm recuperating from a chemical face peel, a procedure done two days ago to remove facial and neck scars caused by melanoma (skin cancer), discovered and removed last year, around the same time as my tiled bathroom was upended by a burst pipe flooding from the unit above me. Fun times.

Today, because I'm to remain prone, head elevated, I spent the entire day and night watching CNN's coverage of what's come to be known as The Capital Insurrection. It's already the first anniversary. I saw hour after hour of video upheaval, accompanied by discussion after discussion of astonishment and outrage, as commentator after commentator searched for meaning: what it means that it happened and what responsible reactions now lay squarely with us ordinary American citizens.

Ironically, today would have been my deceased husband's eighty-second birthday. During phone chats with our three adult kids and the two adult grandchildren, they all individually and laughingly pointed out that this date has gained significantly greater volatility.

As are so many of life's ironies, it's funny, but it's not.

My life partner, the father of my children, was, in fact, a man who craved trouble, who, because of his damaging formative years, coupled with his natural intelligence and inherited manipulative abilities, truly was a storm. In fact, that was one of my quotes for his obituary: "'I married a storm,' said Kimbeth Wehrli Judge."

Here's a Story about Me at Twenty-Four
On my blissfully slow journey to something resembling adulthood, I married a man who assured me we'd finish our college educations together before beginning our family. Turned out he quickly secured his dream job and impregnated

me. Because of my newly developing motherly instincts, we soon moved from our party life in the city to the tranquility of suburban safety.

Accepting my constraints, I began frugally preparing our nest by resurrecting my high school home economics lessons, locating my sewing machine, and creating curtains by measuring and hemming brightly colored sheets.

Intent on mastering this homemaking thing, I also turned to cooking, found an Italian recipe for spaghetti sauce, and set out to the local market. It's a vivid memory still. I'm facing the alphabetically lined wall of spices, clutching my recipe, which states:

- add basil,
- add cilantro,
- add garlic powder,
- add oregano,
- add parsley flakes,
- add salt,
- add freshly ground black pepper,
- add all at once.

All at once? It's not in the As. I figure it must be in a special grouping, such as meat tenderizer, so now I'm staring at the end part of the collection, re-examining each title, wondering if it's somehow coded, sort of like the Dewey decimal system. I'm clearly at a loss, very pregnant, and now really hot, but there's no way I'm leaving.

Eventually, the manager appears quietly by my side to ask if he can help. I'm honestly thrilled to see a kind face, which is when I look down at my recipe to point to the spice I'm hotly pursuing. And I suddenly understand. How could I not have understood? But now I'm rendered speechless with humiliation and can only point to the missing spice.

In a kindness I will never forget, he looks at me, skips a beat, then another, and gently says, "Perhaps this means to gather all the spices and add them at the same time, all at once."

(Tiny beads of sweat have appeared above my upper lip) "OH!" I say, "Oh."

He treats me kindly, as if I were a child, with soothing words, "That's OK. The directions aren't worded well. Shall we locate the canned tomato paste? It's in Aisle 4," he says, as he leads me there.

Now Here's a Story about Me at Seventy-Eight

My husband is newly dead, my children are long ago grown and gone, and I am managing our home alone. I find myself in an *all-at-once* situation, in a recipe for disaster... because how could so many destructive occurrences be happening all at once?

It's enough of a blow to bury my husband:

- add COVID-19 pandemic isolation,
- add not being able to see my kids and my grandchildren,
- add America's children losing years of solid education,
- add political mismanagement,
- add rampant propaganda—our country's allegiance being purposely divided,
- add the botched Afghanistan withdrawal,
- add the insurrection at the United States Capitol,
- add uncontrolled climate change.

The solutions? They're not in my wheelhouse. They're nowhere to be found.

Why would I include the national situation in a book of shared empathy devoted to bringing healthiness to widowhood? Because our safety lies in that wonky imbalance, and reading and listening to the daily news is going to further freak you out unless you understand life's complexities and that humans are erratic in nature. History ebbs and flows. Be calm and cooperate.

"This too shall pass." Consider that this adage applies to both bad and good, so thoroughly enjoy your fun.

Most phases of life require on-the-job training, as does widowhood. Writing about the experience, by comparing my newly widowed existence to that of others, broadened my view into a deeper understanding of the pulsating expansion and contraction of life in general. There's a kind of pleasant stability in accepting a *that's life* attitude. Not all good, not all bad, but fairly equal amounts of both is pretty much the way things go.

Conclusions are often sad, but the one called Death leaves a chasm. Next chapters happen regardless, and newfound contentment is pretty much up to you. It's not easy, and it's not fast. What it is, though, is necessary.

It's necessary:
- to disentangle from grief by getting busy,
- to personalize your own swan song,
- to find your fun and your joy, and live it out gracefully.

Becoming Herself

Kelly Judge Goldberg

My mom's Third Act opened with her caring around the clock for my dying dad. Seemingly unfazed by his declining health and horrific symptoms, and both of their sleeplessnesses, the woman was a vehicle of peace and humor. I'm not exaggerating. Ask around.

Once Bernie was gone, Kimbeth just kept becoming. She worked on her next novel, started while Dad was declining. She gathered widows to share their stories for this anthology, editing and cheering them along.

Mom examined her relationships, determining which ones withstood the test of time, as well as those that required tender loving attention, or even space, to evolve.

She just kept on growing... despite COVID-19, which reared its deadly, isolating head mid-way through our first year of mourning Dad's departure; amidst the social unrest that presented itself on the front lawn of her tucked-away-in-plain-site Chicago condo; no thanks to the self-destructive politics exploding in front of her eyes that were glued to the TV. Remarkably, Mom embraced a generally outward stoicism, as she puzzled through the various stages of her personal grief.

As if all this wasn't challenging enough, my mom's first grandchild's ulcerative colitis worsened. Our son, Danny, was hospitalized three times in eight months and had to take his law school finals at the Mayo Clinic. Danny's *Ahma* provided daily compassion and comfort. She was a permanent fixture of loving strength for all of us during this scary time.

Had Bernie been around, the two of them would have battled semi-privately about all of this. And I mean, battled. Fighting through emotions was their fifty-year history.

But, with Dad gone, Mom had to comprehend her feelings about these exaggerated circumstances without the truth/excuse of Bernie's dramatic navigation of the shit show that was our world, our country, our state, our city, our family.

Empowered by her newfound ability to navigate uncharted rough waters alone with grace and calm, she bloomed MORE.

And here we ARE.

I miss my dad terribly. We were very close. He was a trusted confidante. My forever fan. There are so many ways I aspire to be just like him.

If you would have seen the two of us enjoying one another throughout my life, you'd be surprised by how many times I tried to convince my mom to leave him over the course of their initial thirty years together. Or maybe you wouldn't. It's not like I kept it a secret.

I inherited from Bernie this visceral need to call it like I see it. And while I deeply appreciated how my father encouraged a progressive life for his daughters and then granddaughters, I understood from an early age that, as my mother's traditional husband, Dad possessed some noteworthy deficiencies.

To his credit, somehow my dad was never upset whenever I took my mom's side, which was almost always.

I was also fascinated by his unrelenting loyalty to Mom, conveyed to me even in the middle of one of their days or weeks-long arguments.

I came to understand that Dad's refusal for the two of us to bond against Mom was a demonstration of his FOREVER and FAVORITE love for HER. While that initially annoyed (adolescent) me, I ultimately appreciated it.

I determined that this loyalty was also an unspoken acknowledgment that he drew first blood, not necessarily in their most immediate skirmishes, but certainly from an original sin perspective. And when Dad brought his Chicago Tribune editor, no BS, take-no-prisoners perspective to his honest assessment of his role in our family tumult, it provided me with a sense of security and respect.

Because while Dad was, in fact, the storm Kimbeth described in the eulogy she delivered beautifully at my brother's gorgeous church, luckily for me, Bernie acknowledged that responsibility. Such blessed honesty between father and daughter defined not only our adult relationship, but also the close relationship he enjoyed with my husband and the sacred bond he shared with our children.

So, even though it probably seems crazy strange that I pivoted so quickly while Dad was suddenly dying fast from his Stage 4 pancreatic cancer, I immediately knew that his death made room for his bride to enjoy a Third Act.

My siblings knew it.

My husband and adult-ish kids got it pretty much right away, as well.

Don't misunderstand. He WAS supposed to live well into his nineties, like his father before him. No one had heretofore ever imagined a dead Bernie.

But really, once those who'd had an up-close-and-personal relationship with my parents were able to move beyond their own attachment to Dad and their despair about his critical illness, most were able to comprehend Bernie's death in this expansive way.

And so it is today, in the cozy comfort of her ever-perfected treehouse of a home, Mom is FREE to truly BE.

Kimbeth Ann Wehrli Judge is becoming herself.

Kelly Judge Goldberg
(Daughter of Kimbeth and Bernie Judge)
Kelly Judge Goldberg is a lifelong educator who knows that every moment is a teachable one. She is blessed with Danny and Bella, her fabulous, frank, compassionate, clever twenty-something children. These loves of her life are made possible thanks to her bashert, Michael. Kelly is grateful to share the Judge journey with her siblings BJ and Jessie and additionally thankful for her chosen brother and sisters, all of whom offer slices of clarity, comedy, and love.

Kelly misses her dad, is proud of her mom, and is certain that the lessons of her childhood provide the dynamic blueprint of the life she and Mike keep creating.

Loss Is a Four-Letter Word

Isabella Goldberg

loss is a Four Letter Word

loss is Profane
it is Unfettered and Piercing

loss is Explicit and Vulgar
and Dutifully approved for All audiences

an Irreverent act of the Earthly world
made Supernatural by its
Constant and Bemusing habits

loss is a neat Euphemism for the
Blunt and Rusty blade of death

loss is Four Characters that Tingle
like Phantom limbs

a Shocking single syllable
that can Hold Its Own
with the best of them

Isabella Goldberg
(Granddaughter of Kimbeth and Bernie Judge)

Bella is a proud granddaughter of Kimbeth and Bernie Judge. She is honored to participate in a project with such a wide array of wonderful women. She is glad to help promote the life lessons that can be found in these powerful testimonials from her elders to her peers.

Bella is a first-year student at DePaul University College of Law. Certain of her aspiration to become a legal advocate for individuals with disabilities, but, like so many of her peers, less inclined to be attracted to the idea of marriage.

Adding a third generation of perspective into the mix, she is passionate about learning from her grandmother and mother to synthesize their life lessons into modern-day applicability. The power and strength that come from motherhood and widowhood are universally informative.

And I Am Content

Gail Zelitzky

Part I: Almost from the Time We Met, I Knew Al Would Go First—If Our Marriage Lasted

We were fixed up by mutual friends who, once they saw we were becoming serious, took Al aside and asked him if he knew what he was getting himself into. We enjoyed a good laugh over that. On our second date, we spent the evening describing our first marriages and the dysfunction that both of us experienced. No, we were not abused or physically in danger. We were married to the wrong people. And his four children and my three all exhibited the effects of living under those conditions. My first marriage lasted fifteen years, Al's for twenty-six!

There were many things against Al's and my relationship from the start. I had three dependent children. When he learned that, the first date almost didn't happen. My first son, going on fourteen, was living at the inpatient hospital for a three-year stay at the Menninger Foundation in Topeka, KS. My second son was eight and my daughter was soon to be fifteen.

Al's four kids were already on their own, except for the youngest, who briefly lived with his mother. That boy was in the same high school in the same year as my daughter. Al was also fifteen years older than I was. I recently asked my

57

stepdaughter if our age difference had bothered her. She said it never had. I was grateful for her acceptance.

Al and I discovered so many things in common, from jogging to tennis; an overwhelming desire for intimacy; from intellectual pursuits to work, travel, and the cultural arts. The relationship was magical, and nothing was going to pull us apart from each other. Al's ability to deal with the constant tensions of our home situation was testimony to his love for me. As for me, I had found the love of my life. Nine months after our first date, we married in a lovely, small ceremony at my parent's condominium, in the company of friends and family. Miraculously, all the children attended the ceremony and managed to get along–at least on that one night.

The relationships among the children, and ours with them, proved taxing. Yet our personal relationship flourished. I look back on that time and wonder, how was that possible? One reason was our mutual respect. I was working full time when we met, and he supported and encouraged it.

We both loved to cook and took turns making dinner right from the start. We loved to entertain. My parents, who willingly cared for my children while they were young, made it possible to travel and we often combined our love of food with visits to locations in different countries known for their culinary treasures. I have so many fond memories of our adventures.

In 1989, Al's oldest son died of a massive heart attack, at thirty-eight, while sitting at the kitchen table with his mother. That same year, only nine years after we married, Al's personal physician called and said, "What we used to call hepatitis non-A–non-B because we didn't know there were other variations and genotypes, now has a name. You have hepatitis C."

Al was destined to experience chronic hep-C for the rest of his life. A few new drugs were discovered that caused temporary remission, and he tried them all. However, not everyone responded equally, and none led to a cure. Eventually, his condition resulted in cirrhosis of the liver and a breakdown of the pancreas and kidneys. He never discovered how he acquired this dreadful disease—he could remember no blood transfusions or other needles and had not been a drinker. It was an extremely painful way to die.

While hepatitis C used to be a lifelong condition, happily, today, there are excellent drug choices to defeat the many genotypes. The earlier people are diagnosed, the better the outcomes.

In 2009, twenty-nine years after we married, when I was sixty-eight, Al died peacefully at home surrounded by family. This man, who loved life so vigorously, was gone at eighty-two. Our relationship had proved the test of time.

Part II: If I've Learned Anything from All This, It Is the Knowledge That It's Not Over until It's Over!

Much of our marriage was spent dealing with this chronic illness: the last few years often played out in emergency rooms around the city, pushing a wheelchair or simply expecting that this was the moment he would die. You'd think I'd have been totally prepared to experience life without him. We even assured each other before we married that if we enjoyed ten good years together, we would be grateful. Yet, until the moment he died, I never had to do that–live without him. And the reality is that it was so much harder than I ever imagined.

In 1987, we moved into a large three-bedroom condominium on Lake Shore Drive. Every time we walked into that magnificent building, we pinched ourselves. Both of us grew up at times poor, mostly middle class, and, so, remained forever thankful for our good fortune. Living across the street from the park and minutes away from Lake

Michigan appealed to our love of walking, playing tennis, and, for me, biking.

The exterior environment suited me well. Nevertheless, once he died, the interior of the apartment suddenly became huge. There were no children in the house and no pets. I couldn't find a place for myself. Nowhere did I feel comfortable. The room where we watched television was unbearable to be in by myself. (Perhaps, because it was also the room we set up for him while in hospice at home.)

I've worked from home since 2000. When Al retired, however, he set up his office space in the same room. I'd preferred he hadn't, yet now, when his desk sat empty, I longed for his presence and the inconvenience of his being there, in the same room where I spent so much of my time each day. The house was empty, silent, and I felt utterly alone. It was the first time in my entire life that I lived entirely on my own.

I always expected to be a teacher. However, marriage at nineteen and an immediate miscarriage followed by a full-term pregnancy derailed that course. I earned my undergraduate degree three months after my daughter was born. Her first brother followed in quick order and proved to be a handful from the day he arrived, so I never made good use of my teaching certificate. My second son was born five years after his brother.

Life was terribly chaotic when my first husband left us. We were financially bereft, and I had no way to support my little family. Within weeks after he bailed, everything got worse. Now my first son became even more violent, his mental illness peaking, and I feared for all our lives. Therapy had been an ongoing attempt since he was four. He was kicked out of every school he attended, and by this point, we were out of options. An in-patient setting seemed the only hope.

Because I flew to Topeka once a month for three days

while taking care of the two at home (again, thanks to my parents), I required great flexibility. Teaching was no longer an option, nor was working for an employer in any capacity. Consequently, when my father invited me into his business, I knew I had to accept.

I always said I received a doctorate in business, working with him. He was the most creative businessperson I knew. I am still grateful to him for the opportunity. I ran the company for seventeen years and, when we sold the business, built a second and third enterprise in the same industry. For the last twenty-three years, I switched gears altogether and began consulting small business owners and coaching women business owners to grow successfully while attempting to maintain some sense of balance.

Life is a never-ending shift from good to bad and back to good. My own world has been a series of ups and downs alongside roaring success. Mine is the story of living a life seeing the glass half full, and how I learned that tiny shifts in perspective create huge results. Now that I am eighty, I understand my story was my own doing. I'm no longer so emotional.

Creativity has always been at the heart of my career. When I became a widow, I knew, more than ever, that it was time for me to think creatively if I was going to take the sting out of the unhappy circumstance I found myself in. I knew, too, that I had to find my way back to resilience so that I could create a new life that was worth living.

I worked daily to retain a positive approach and a positive attitude. I journaled. I wrote about what happened each day that was good. What did I want to change? And what kind of future did I envision for myself? Shifts occur when creative thinking exists, and that requires a mindset that is willing to stretch, conceive the unbelievable, and accept that all things are possible. I found myself asking, "In what ways might I apply this type of thinking to me?" "What crossroads am I at right now?" "Am I on the alert to focus on possibilities?"

I knew I could. I had already reinvented myself many times. Though, if you had been there night after night, seeing me dissolve in tears, you might have wondered, was I kidding myself? I was very emotional all my life, quick to tear up. I think I cried for (mostly privately) the first two years after Al died. Still, it didn't keep me from reaching out to friends and plotting my future. The positive side of my nature helped me to continue engaging with friends. The first year, I had plenty to keep me busy, including cleaning up our financial affairs and Al's belongings and pushing myself to maintain an active social life. It was the second year when the reality of being alone and needing to carve out a new life really hit.

I decided I could sit for two of my grandchildren on Fridays after school. They were still quite young and that would shorten the weekend, brighten my week, give their parents time for themselves, and build a foundation for an ongoing relationship with them. I did that for many years until they moved out of state. Another loss, but now I had a place to visit to get away from Chicago winters. And the foundation we built has made it possible to maintain a long-distance relationship with them.

The onset of widowhood was difficult for me. I had to push beyond the sadness and reality of being alone and open my heart and mind to new ways of being and thinking. I do love a challenge. This new way of living turned out to enhance my love of adventure because now I had to find it for myself. I didn't know what I didn't know. Other single women became my role models. I asked questions and worked hard to maintain a curiosity about how to make life better.

I soon realized the right path for me was to return to school and complete the master's degree I started when I was first divorced. This time, I was determined. My obligations were different; my work was going well, and it was an important pursuit to cross off my bucket list. It would get me away from thinking about myself to learning something new. At seventy-four, six years after taking the plunge, I matriculated, earning a MAAPS degree (Master of Arts in Applied Professional Studies), from DePaul University. Had I been younger, with more disposable income, I would have pursued a doctorate. Academia had always been in the back of my mind to pursue teaching children's literature. I never accomplished that, but I did write a children's book, called *Patches* (Silver-Robins, 2013), about acceptance and safety and love. The purpose of these studies was to better understand creativity and innovation to help entrepreneurs grow. I didn't know at the time how much it would also help me in life.

In its simplest form, creativity is coming up with ideas; innovation is doing something with those ideas. Breakthrough thinking is the result that identifies a new process, discovers new inventions, helps you communicate better, creates new revenue streams, and offers a unique type of service.

In life, we face decisions every day, some of which impact important issues. We experience an endless barrage of crises, interventions, and, yes, ordinary conversations—all of which influence the outcomes we seek. Not all decisions are life-changing. Some are small and easily made. What should I have for dinner? Is that a play worth seeing? My friend invited me to join her on a trip. Should I go?

Others are more complex. Is now a good time to move and where? When will, or should, I retire? Should I consider looking at retirement facilities? If I can't do everything exactly the way I'd like to do it, what are my options? Creative problem-solving helps me think more critically so that I recognize my underlying motives better and make smarter decisions.

In my current life, I continue to work, and a few years ago became a podcaster. My weekly show, *Women Over 70: Aging Reimagined*, interviews women aged from seventy to over one hundred. My podcast partner and co-host was my faculty mentor at DePaul. If I had not aspired to get my degree, we would never have met or embarked on this exciting venture together. Our vision is to shatter the myth that women become irrelevant as they age. The hundreds of women we've interviewed, between the ages of seventy and over one hundred, dispel that notion. These women are my new role models, reinforcing for me that learning, purpose, and gratitude make life exciting, challenging, and rewarding. I look forward to new adventures in my eighties.

Becoming a widow spurred me on to remain interesting, be visible and keep learning, stay involved in current events, and advocate for others. I began to find other single women who are on their own living rich lives, and who fill my life with joy. Yes, a few old friends disappeared, and too many, sadly, have passed away, but my new friends of all ages are viable companions with whom I socialize, travel, attend cultural events, dine with, walk with, and talk with. I'm lucky to have friendships that formed fifty, even sixty years ago. These are the friends who are there for me when life gets me down. Talking helps me cope with the inevitable family tragedies, illness, and bumps along the way.

At our age, we can be true to ourselves. There is nothing to hide or leave unsaid. I can look at my life now and accept it did not turn out exactly as I hoped. And then I look at all the good in my life. If you are lucky enough to have children and grandchildren, life is even richer. I have one son and one stepdaughter that I count on, along with dear cousins, a niece and nephew, and grandchildren.

If I'm honest, in the twelve years I've been widowed, I've discovered I prefer living on my own at this time of my life. I've tried online dating. It does nothing for me. Do I miss the intimacy of a loving relationship? Yes, I do. Yet, I plan to continue living independently until it is no longer feasible. I've always felt independent, but was more dependent than I knew.

With all the ups and downs of my life, some might wonder how I find so much joy and feel so grateful. Despite several bouts of cancer, other surgeries, and chronic illnesses, I remain in reasonably good health. My brain is (mostly) working fine. I do worry I will outlive my money, but I have options. And every day I know that tomorrow is still to come. Another adventure waits for me. And I am content.

Gail Zelitzky
(widowed thirteen years)
Gail married at nineteen and divorced fifteen years later with three children. She married for the second time in 1980. Al was the love of her life. They experienced twenty-nine remarkable years together before he died in 2009. Gail sees her life as a series of vignettes, each role requiring new skills and learning. Travel, work, continuing education—all endlessly fascinate her. They frame her values, career, and unstoppable resilience.

She continues to work at age eighty. In 2019, she launched *Women Over 70: Aging Reimagined*, a weekly podcast and program. Gail is full of wonder at her own and other women's abilities to continually recreate themselves.

Our Souls Apart

Celina Edelstein

I held him in my arms and felt my heart beating against a limp and heavy, still-warm body. And as I lay him down gently, his face embodied a calm and peaceful repose. He appeared to be sleeping deeply, though with partially closed eyes. A few feet away, a man stood waiting to take my Angelo to the morgue. He told me I could take my time saying goodbye. How does one say goodbye to a soulmate who is no longer here? Does he hear me, see me, feel my presence? Or is there just a nothingness, a void for him? My emotions and my thoughts were completely disoriented, and all I could do was hold his hand, intertwining my fingers with his. This was our nightly reverie of love just before we fell asleep next to each other, a symbol of our souls resting together with expectant morning risings to share another new day.

But there would no longer be new days with Angelo, so part of my soul went with him that morning. There would be no goodbyes, but only a hope that our souls would reunite in the future. Since part of my soul was with him now, I would be free of pain and grief. Or so I thought.

When I was young, in my teens, and dreaming about my future, I knew that this future would have to include science as part of my life. As a student in high school, I was very much attracted to chemistry and decided I would focus on that and other related sciences. Science would then encompass the direction of my life's path. My college education partially fulfilled those dreams and introduced me to scientific research. From then, I was hooked.

As in any dream, there are side roads that one takes that may be off the beaten track, but somehow, eventually, lead you onto the right path to truly realize your dreams and more. In my case, it took some time. On that side road, I met and married a man. We were both fresh out of college. He was starting medical school, and I was the sole breadwinner. I worked in medical research, which at least kept my dreams partially alive. We moved from New York to Chicago, where my husband was to begin his medical internship at the University of Chicago.

In the fall of 1963, the first time I met Angelo, my life changed forever. I was twenty-five years old and looking for a research position at the university. Angelo was awarded a new research grant and was starting his new laboratory and looking for research assistants. I found him to be very amiable and charming and, as he described his research projects, I felt his enthusiasm deeply and knew this was going to be a most important adventure.

Accepting the position, I spent the next week delving into the field of lipoproteins, their structure and function, and their clinical relevance to heart disease. My energy and interest were boundless. I was in charge of equipping this lab with instruments, chemicals, etc., and setting up original new experiments under Angelo's guidance. He made me a partner in solving the mysteries of this science. Thus we began together, and over time expanded the lab with national and international scientists and created a world-renowned center for lipoprotein research, culminating in new original discoveries. Our lab published hundreds of peer-reviewed papers and received many national and international awards. Angelo became my mentor, teacher, and best friend. Throughout our journey, we could read each other's minds and would frequently finish sentences the other started.

Our personal lives were different. I was married and had a son, but I got divorced after thirteen years and Angelo, who was fourteen years older than I, was happily married with two children. We socialized frequently and knew each other's families. Unfortunately, three years before Angelo's retirement, his wife passed away due to cancer.

Somehow, so close to retirement and slowly closing down our lab, we found ourselves adrift in our sadness and loneliness, and not knowing how our final days would turn out. We started dating and found an attraction we never realized existed. In a way, it was quite comical being so involved in our research. We treated and interacted with each other differently in those times than now. Maybe all these years, I unconsciously regarded him as a fatherly mentor and never realized how close we really were.

In 2011, after forty-eight years of working together, we decided to close the lab and retire together. We bought a condo downtown, traveled, laughed a lot, and loved each other. I had never known such happiness could exist on this earth. We had so much of our past in common that our thoughts intertwined and became one.

On the morning of Friday, January 12, 2018, Angelo got up and took his temperature. He was not feeling well, fighting a cold that persisted for a week and his lower eyelids were red and irritated. Although he had no fever, he was not himself and I suggested we see the ophthalmologist to check his eyes. I was washing up in my bathroom and he was getting ready in his. As I finished dressing, I became aware of an unusual stillness in the house and walked into the hallway bathroom, only to find Angelo lying on the floor with a pool of blood encircling his head. I tried to lift him and, seeing that he was unresponsive, I quickly called for the paramedics.

While waiting for them, I was pacing back and forth in total disbelief and shock. It was as if my mind was disconnected from my body, and all I could feel was fear and a terrible ache in my heart. I was losing Angelo, and I was totally helpless. Then the medics came, gave him oxygen, and tried very hard to keep him alive with IV fluids, drugs, intubation, and finally, CPR, which lasted at least fifteen minutes with no response. During this interval, I called his son in California, and we both prayed and cried together as the final verdict was given. The coroner came, and then he was placed in the hallway on a blanket and I lay holding him before the gurney arrived to take him away.

That night in bed, I reached over to seek his hand, only to find empty space. Suddenly, as if on cue, I heard Angelo's voice, loud and clear, calling my name. I jumped up, only to find darkness. Was this his final goodbye? Or did we connect for eternity?

The following few days and weeks were a complete blur to me, and, thanks to Angelo's son and a few close friends, I somehow got through it. It was a time of sleepless nights, binging on television series till three or four in the morning, then showering, eating almost nothing, and preparing for memorial talks with the University, honoring Angelo and exhibits of his work at the Museum of Medical Science, and writing his memorial articles with colleagues for various professional journals.

My life's journey with Angelo not only fulfilled my dreams of being a scientist but also introduced me to a man who became my soulmate. We had known each other for a total of fifty-five years, which included fun, laughter, tears, joy and enthusiasm, discovery and excitement, trust, interest and constant learning, hope and love. All the emotions that life can experience, we shared until we were as one. I could not have wished for a better experience with any other human being. Now, in the winter of my life, I can rejoice in my memories of Angelo and shed tears when I miss him, but also have hope that I can reunite our souls when we meet each other again.

It has now been over three years since Angelo and I parted, and it feels like I was just with him yesterday. The pain of loss is still there, and I think of him every day. I can't seem to let go of my emotions, nor do I really want to. Because if I do, I fear I would be lost and live without purpose. But time and life go on, and I am content living in the condo we shared. I have made good friends, some who knew Angelo and new ones that did not, and socialize frequently with them. I continue to participate in the book club, reading many books, including those on politics and foreign policy that I took part in with the League of Women Voters, and keep up with scientific journals. Before COVID-19, in late 2019, I traveled to Singapore and Viet Nam. Due to an unfortunate accident in Viet Nam, I broke my leg and returned home cutting my trip short. In some way, I was happy that Angelo did not have to see me in this condition, but at the same time, I would have loved for him to give me his helping hand and assurances. My relationship with his son continues to grow stronger and we visit each other a few times a year since he lives in California. Being with his son brings me closer to Angelo, and we often reminisce about him with love and laughter. I know it makes both of us feel that much closer to each other and him.

When COVID-19 arrived in 2020, all our lives changed. The time was ripe for being alone, to rethink calmly about my place in this world without Angelo. I have found peace in my sorrow and am more at ease with my thoughts of him, though I still long to feel his touch just one last time. I can now smile, for the memory of him rekindles our love for each other and illuminates the wonderful life we shared.

For the present, I continue to socialize with my friends, read voraciously and exercise more with long walks, gym workouts, and yoga. I am contemplating changing my living environment by moving to a community in another state that has a warmer climate. But that would mean leaving the home that Angelo and I shared and all the memories infused with it, a task much too hard to bear, at least for now. I am fortunate in that I found a deep love I believe only happens once in a lifetime: it fulfilled my dreams of a scientific life and intertwined it with the love and soul of another human being.

Celina Edelstein
(widowed four years)
Celina's first marriage of thirteen years was a time when her husband was in medical school, interning and fulfilling a residency in Radiology, while she was working in a biomedical research lab, building her career and raising their son. After divorcing, she raised their son to be educated and to become an attorney, all the while involved in her research, publishing papers, traveling the globe, and being recognized in her field.

Upon retirement, Celina's mentor and Director of Research, Angelo (now widowed), and Celina began a new life together, traveling, moving to a new home, and both discovering new happiness. After living together for seven years, Angelo passed away. Devastated, Celina found herself alone and trying to make a new life again.

Now she has renewed herself. She's made a new group of friends and partakes in social activities, is effectively involved in her book club, and has resumed traveling.

She spends time with her son and her two grandchildren, who are about to start college. At the ripe age of eighty-three, she has had the opportunity to look back at her life and is now writing her memoir.

Twice Widowed

Naomi Stern

Part A

When I was nineteen years old and about to leave Greenwich Village in New York City for an industrial city in the Midwest, my mother asked me a sensible question. "Do you love him?"

It was an unforgettable moment. "I don't really know what love is," was my response.

Looking back over time, at my impetuous decision to leave New York, friends, and family ties, I have come to see the word *love* representing an evolutionary process. My first marriage was full of the hormones of youth. We isolated ourselves from our families and built pseudo-family units of new friends. Most importantly, we both wanted our children. We two became parents (four in eight years). It was not always easy, but love did evolve. It took shape on camping trips (even the one in a hurricane on Cape Cod), fishing excursions, visiting museums, seeing theater and movies, and more. Every night, all of us would gather at bedtime to sing together. Our repertoire went from lullabies to cowboy ballads. My husband and I had shared enthusiasms.

As can be expected, there were quarrels, but we stuck to our rule that we would never go to sleep angry. We weathered scary times, like the McCarthy period of the fifties and the protests to end the Vietnam War. My husband became a draft counselor. However, the result of these stresses was a tight bond that gained strength over time. Friends called us "the fortress family". Love grew as we grew. It came from our commitment to each other and to our family.

Sadly, my husband died at the age of sixty-three. Somehow, my own youth died with him. I lost many memories of my nineteen-year-old self, young parenthood, and new friendships. I had to find my way into adulthood without him at my side.

Several years later, I reconnected with an old friend. He was a person very different from my first husband. He was a businessman, but his love was photography. Where my first husband loved language, writing poetry and short stories, this man was a visual artist. He saw beauty, humor, and good design in a piece of wood or found object. Through him, I learned to see differently.

We had no children in common, so we were free to lead a life of joyous adventure. Many trips were focused on bird watching. He and I were very competitive, and as a result, we learned a lot about birding.

Because we were older, we found ways to accommodate each other's needs without the drama of our youth. I learned to wait when I felt a problem arise. Soon we could both see things from each other's perspective and share our points of view.

Looking back as I write this, I can see how my two loves were different, but also very much alike. We shared a love of theater, movies, museums, and travel. We also were interested in and loved to discuss political issues of the day.

Now that I am just ninety-two years old, I still can only approach a sensible meaning to the word *love*. I know it is a feeling that deepens, if you are lucky, with time. It means something different as you age because you are different. The experience of being a parent and part of a family unit contrasts with the freedom of being a couple with many choices open.

I loved both of my husbands, each in a way befitting my age and extent of life experience.

Part B

I have a prejudice against the phrase "He passed," or, "She passed away." These phrases are meant to mean "he/she died." Some psychologists believe that we Americans have such fear of the process that ends all life that we find the word *died* rude or hurtful.

In contrast to this American attitude, I learned of and found myself intrigued with the holiday called the *Day of the Dead,* celebrated in many Latinx communities. My son Paul and I spent time at the Mexican Fine Arts Museum in Chicago, learning more about the meaning of that day. Once, in a light rain, as we left the museum and were passing a large paved area, we saw many family groups celebrating the holiday. Colorful blankets lay on the ground to delineate a private space. On it, the family created small altars containing religious objects, food, photos, trinkets, etc. These represented their loved one in life. Each area was unique and personal.

Later on, I commented that I wished people could attend their own memorials before they died so they could laugh and cry as people told funny or serious stories about the deceased. At that time, both my and both my husbands' parents, as well as many friends, had died. Memorial events always impressed me. One often learned things about the deceased that they never knew. There were wonderful stories and important reviews of the meaning of the person's life. I remember thinking that maybe someday I would be able to attend my own memorial.

Then came my eighty-fifth birthday. My family gathered (all of us a big crowd) in my Indiana house. I had no idea what was going to occur, but I was sent down to the basement. Finally, I was called upstairs. As I entered the living room, I saw a giant *ofrenda*, or altar, which consisted of a large rectangle containing small shelves and other spaces, all covered with green felt. Yellow flowers were set in place. Special objects were placed within, such as a teacup with a tea bag, a bottle of rum, lit candles, black Chuckles, a brassiere, family photos, etc.

Each of my four children explained their contribution to the *ofrenda* as each object expressed my relationship with them. One son displayed a rabbit that is a lump of painted clay that he made with me when he was three years old. He explained that working with his hands in a creative way has been with him ever since. A granddaughter brought a little quilt I had helped her make when she was young. My daughter read two poems.

With laughter and even tears—alive and well—I happily experienced my memorial in the form of the *Day of the Dead*.

I have had a lucky life.

July of 2022
An addition regarding a precious addition...

Pete Seeger sang a song called *Turn, Turn, Turn.* I've always loved it. Interestingly, Pete Seeger's lyrics are taken straight from the Bible, the only additions being the word, 'TURN,' and the last line in his song.

Ecclesiastes 3:1-8 (Darby Translation)

[1]To everything there is a season, and a time to every purpose under the heavens:

[2]A time to be born, and a time to die; A time to plant, and a time to pluck up that which is planted;

[3]A time to kill, and a time to heal; A time to break down, and a time to build up;

[4]A time to weep, and a time to laugh; A time to mourn, and a time to dance;

[5]A time to cast away stones, and a time to gather stones together; A time to embrace, and a time to refrain from embracing;

[6]A time to seek, and a time to lose; A time to keep, and a time to cast away;

[7]A time to rend, and a time to sew; A time to keep silence, and a time to speak;

[8]A time to love, and a time to hate; A time of war, and a time of peace.

Turn! Turn! Turn! was written by Pete Seeger (1919-2014) in 1959.

I am now ninety-three years old and have had the joys of spring and the sadness of death.

I have found new joy, and, in a sense, re-birth, in Rose, my great-granddaughter. I last saw her at a month old. Of course, she was beautiful with a sweet mouth, long eyelashes, and arched eyebrows. Her tiny hands and feet, and amazing tiny nails, entranced me. Sweet Rose.

There *is* a time for every season. My greatest joy was seeing how happy her parents, aunts, uncle, and grandparents were. My son, the grandfather, shed tears of joy!

I felt sad that my husband, who died at sixty-three, could not share in this new season. It was at that moment that this song came back to me, the words forever relevant, and the tune so beautifully calming.

Naomi Stern
(widowed twelve years)

Naomi's young first marriage involved the crazy, fun life of raising four children. She was widowed at age sixty-three, and eleven years later married businessman and photographer, Jack Jaffe, who died in 2010. Naomi spends her time creating pottery at her home in Indiana, embroidering and quilting in her Chicago condominium, occasionally traveling to New York City for family time with her children and grandchildren, and now, her great-grandchild, Rose. For her, being with friends is a high priority, and humor is essential. She enjoys a yearly trip abroad and has been on seven continents, some as a widow.

Jimmy One-Lung

Jane Hyde Hasil

Looking back, I was a widow long before Jim passed away. Marriage is a crap shoot at best—if you get lucky, and work hard at it, it can be wonderful.

Jim was a wild child, and I was a preppie. But I was attracted to his ongoing wacky sense of humor. As an example, this was his response to his lung removal back in 2014. "Well," he said. "Now I guess you can call me 'Jimmy One-Lung'."

With all he eventually went through, he only lost his humor for a bit during chemo, when he was very, very ill. During that time, I became Jim's caregiver. For the first time in my life, I wasn't the kids' mom, not Jim's wife, not just me—I was the line to Jim's life.

In January 2015, Jim was recuperating from two laminectomies (surgical removal of the posterior arch of a vertebra) performed in October 2014, and from a right pneumonectomy (removal of his entire right lung due to cancer) in December 2014. He was so ill that we didn't go to Biloxi for the winter. We were just at home, going to appointments, seeing doctors, dispensing medicines, and keeping Jim as comfortable as possible. He went into chemo in January and finished in April 2015.

During his illness, I started taking over more jobs, with Jim's help, of course. I learned to become comfortable driving the 2500 Chevy pickup truck. Being an auto mechanic by career, Jim made me learn about it all. From stem to stern. And he taught me to identify what we could not fix and where to take it to get the job done. Come October 2015, the chemo had failed to hold his lung cancer from growing, so Jim had radiation through November 2015. We were hopeful that this would be the miracle we sought.

In December 2015, a year into Jim's illness, he could still drive the truck and pull our thirty-seven-foot, fifth-wheel trailer down to Biloxi, Mississippi, for the 2015-16 winter. We had a duplicate set of doctors down in Biloxi, and it was there, in March 2016, that he started to need supplemental oxygen at night, and was diagnosed with CHF (congestive heart failure) and COPD (chronic obstructive pulmonary disease). These additional diagnoses, on top of lung cancer and one remaining lung, made him a lot weaker. At this point, I needed to help him get into the truck. I'd get into what I named my "Dick Butkus" stance, put my shoulder under his buns, and lift while he pulled. That did the trick. I did all the driving.

By April 2016, we enlisted the help of our son, Ray, who flew down to Biloxi from Midway Airport in Chicago to Gulfport International in Mississippi. He helped us prepare the trailer for the trip home, then drove Jim and me as passengers in the truck back north to Lyons, Illinois. That was such a godsend because I could only handle pulling the trailer in a straight line... no turns for rest areas or food. Ray was experienced at pulling the trailer, and we sure appreciated his help.

When it came time to go back down in November 2016, we asked for Ray's help to pull the trailer and help us set up for the winter. Ray brought his middle daughter Kenna to be his co-pilot/secretary. Our daughter Steffanie drove down in Ray's van with Jim and me as passengers along with two electric carts, two walkers, a portable oxygen concentrator, fifteen tanks of oxygen, and all his meds. No real change in Jim… just a general increase in weakness and difficulty breathing. By this time, I had taken over the finances and all the ordering of pills. Well, what an eye-opener that was.

So now I'm the driver, maintenance manager of the trailer (handling propane for heat, plumbing, sewer), CPA, pharmacist, and nurse. Jim was still receiving immunotherapy every two weeks for his lung cancer and the Opdivo® was doing a good job of keeping the cancer at bay. With the advent of 24/7 oxygen, CHF, and COPD, we asked Ray to return with our truck to pull the trailer home in April 2017. Kenna came with him, and Steffanie and Laney (Steff's youngest daughter) rode along to man the return van to carry Jim and me and all the equipment back up North to Illinois.

Come November 2017, Ray and Kenna pulled the trailer down to Biloxi, with Steff, Jim, and me following in the van. Jim had become increasingly weak but still managed to be a pretty good traveler, despite my having to monitor his breathing constantly. By spring 2018, I had to stay very close to him, which took a great toll on my freedom and free time. And that's when the guilt of feeling tied down really hit me. Yes, friends often offered to "give me a break," but I just couldn't take the chance of an event occurring during someone else's watch. Let's face it, breathing and the need for oxygen immediately is so basic and urgent that it's not like having to give pills at a certain time or feeding someone. It was my responsibility, and I didn't pass it on to anyone else.

In November 2018, Ray and Kenna, and his oldest daughter, Bailee, pulled the trailer back down south to Biloxi. Steff drove a van with me and Jim and the equipment— which included, by now, the O2 tanks in case the portable went down, plus extra O2 lines, masks, and nebulizer. Ray, in the truck, had the BIG 02 concentrator, the BIG O2 tank (three feet tall, which I called BIG Bertha), the walkers, etc. At that point, I could have run a logistics business, but it was all necessary equipment.

It is now January 2019. Jim's immunotherapy stopped keeping his cancer from growing. At this point, the patient is removed from being eligible to receive this relatively new but efficient-to-a-point therapy. Jim was so weak that he could no longer do the three stairs up to the master bedroom nor the three stairs down to the truck without help from Biloxi's finest, the Fire Department Assist Lift group. So we entered into hospice after a few days in the hospital in February 2019 for heart issues. Once in hospice, I was so relieved to have people to talk to immediately if Jim had an issue, to oversee his medicine changes, and to to tend to Jim physically. He was sleeping most of the time, and his eating (what little he did) was about down to his beloved fried egg sandwiches and, the favorite of all, milkshakes.

We had some arguments about his inability to eat, and I was so frustrated that I lost my temper at times. I still cry about that anger I felt back then. But I never cried in front of Jim.

Add cheerleader to that list of hats I was wearing. I feel that I kept him in fine spirits with my creative answers to his question: "Am I dying?"

"Jim, we're all dying every day, but we continue to do the best we can."

He never asked for more of an explanation and would carry on in his usual cheerful manner.

Jim was no longer on most medicines. He had pain in his back and, as long as he was seated or lying down, he was comfortable. *No pain* was the biggest help to me in keeping Jim happy. He really never complained and was always showing concern for me. He actually rallied down south, so that when we came back to Illinois in late March 2019, he had had a great trip. *We* had had a great trip. For this last return, it was Steff as the driver, with me, Jim, Bailee, and Laney as passengers. A full house of relatives coming to the aid of the patriarch. During that trip home, he ate everything, drank root beer, and was happy as a clam for a dying man.

Back home in April 2019, Jim never left our second-floor apartment. Lyons Fire Department carried him up the stairs to his beloved comfy office chair in front of his computer. He was well acquainted with them, although he said it was a scary ride up the stairs. He started using his walker a lot to go the short distance from the bedroom to his computer. I'd find him at three a.m. sitting at his desk, eating a doughnut or some fruit that I'd leave for him in case he got up. I had a monitor connected from his room to mine so that I could keep tabs on him. He hardly ever left the computer room, but on one midnight raid for potato chips, he took his walker through the kitchen into the back pantry, lost his balance while trying to sit in his walker, and fell. We live in a big farmhouse divided into two flats, so Jim's fall alerted Steff's dog downstairs, who barked a lot and woke Steff, who came up and woke me up because I hadn't heard a thing. Out of all of us, only Steff's little dog, Laila, had heard and responded to Jim's tapping his cane for help by barking us all awake. The Fire Department came to lift him up and put him into bed. Once they had left, Jim called me and asked, as he sat on the bed, "Do you think I can have those chips now?"

A checkup showed no broken bones, but he was laid up in bed for a few days. This was about two weeks before he really became weakened. He was still himself, with his mind working pretty much as usual, still funny, still telling me he loved me many times a day and telling his family the same. It wasn't until three days before he died that his full mind wasn't there anymore. He became very childlike, but was still pleased with those milkshakes. That was a Saturday—his last milkshake. On Sunday, he slept most of the day, but he recognized his sister and nephew.

I ordered a hospital bed on Sunday. It was delivered on Monday at noon. One last time, we had the Lyons Fire Department come over to take him from the bedroom to the hospital bed in the computer room. By Tuesday noon, he had slept peacefully away. He was weary, and he went home to rest.

After being the "everything" for Jim for so long, I had a hard time finding my old identity. My body kept going into alert mode. It's hard to explain, but I would awaken at night after hearing him call my name. Then I'd have to get up and look around to make sure it wasn't true. I heard his voice. It was him calling me. But not from here.

I think I'm a much more confident person than I was before Jim's illnesses. I know I learned a lot about life and about what's really important. Jim became so loving through his illness, and I never loved him as much as when he desperately needed me. My family was my rock, and Jim made a big impact on their lives. He was certainly a character that made us laugh a lot and won't be forgotten.

My friends for the past ten years from down south were so supportive of us in Biloxi. They are from all over the States, and I love them like family, and that goes for all my long-time Chicago friends, from where I worked for thirty-two years, and in some cases dating back to 1950.

I'm in the process of learning how to react to things that happen to me, or to events that I am invited to. I lost all forms of spontaneity in October 2014, but it's coming back to me. I felt such relief when Jim died because he was finally at peace and at rest. But I had an overwhelming feeling of "what do I do now?", now that I'm not on call 24/7 as I had been for so long. It took me months for my mind to relax totally. The issue of spontaneity or the ability to plan something in the future is coming back to me now, five months after Jim's passing.

I miss Jim every day, but I thank him for being the best patient I have ever seen… and for ultimately showing me how much I was loved.

Honestly, I also feel a sense of relief and freedom from all the trauma at the end.

I wasn't planning on writing a sequel to my caregiver life with my husband. At the urging of my conscience, however, I feel I should acknowledge a new part of my current life as a seasoned widow.

On second thought, though, I have decided that I'll just keep my new Secret Life portion of living to myself, and just add it to all the great and wonderful things I learned from Jim.

Or:

Here's my take on all that's out-of-whack right now in our current world   ignore what I cannot possibly control.

Life is to be lived, enjoyed passionately, and shared whenever possible, and I'm doing just that.

Jane Hyde Hasil
(widowed three years)

Jane and Jim were married for fifty-two years. Together, they raised two children who produced five granddaughters before Jim passed in 2019.

Jane attended the University of Illinois, majoring in Spanish with a minor in Russian, which became a useful client communication skill later on in her career.

Children came quickly, so she became a stay-at-home mother for nine years before joining a close-to-home insurance agency as a commercial lines agent with a CIC degree in insurance and then spent the next thirty-two years there.

In their spare time, she and Jim boated on the Great Lakes for twenty years before becoming land lubbers, RV-ing between Illinois and Mississippi (which is where Jane still spends the winter season as a snowbird).

Now going into her thirteenth year in the South, her Cajun neighbors at her park are her second family. Jim spent his last four and a half years continuing to go down South to enjoy the Gulf and Jane continues to winter there by herself but not alone, thanks to her Cajun family.

Take Care of Him

Isabella Goldberg

Take care of him, my
Mother said to me about my
brother when I was six and
he was eight and
He pushed a girl
Off the swings, little
boys just don't
Know better

With a vow, I said yes,
Sir, I am patience, I am kindness,
I am here and you are
Loved unconditionally—despite and
Because of your missteps and mistakes and
Fuckups and
one day you will
Be better

Like my mother, I married a
Strong man a
Resilient man a man
Worth the stay but
unlike my mother

I saw the truth in my
own courage and chose to
Love better

In the eyes of my son, I saw
My father and
My brother and
My husband and for them and for
Me I said to him,
"be better."

And when I can shine my light upon
Him no more,
And It becomes time to
Learn and
Live and
Love
Passionately enough to fuel
My own flame I will do so,
Just, better.

And Then There Was One

Sharon Rossman Hirschfeld

I met my husband on a blind date during my freshman year of college. We were young and immediately fell for each other. He was seven years older than I was and ready to settle down. He had just gotten out of the Navy and was attending a business college. We found it interesting that both his and my parents also happened to be seven years apart. In addition, our birthdays were one day and seven years apart. These details made the decision for me. He was my Prince Charming, and I was his Little Princess. I told him that even though he was my Mr. Right, finishing school was very important to me. He could either wait until I graduated to get married or if we married right away, he had to guarantee that I would also earn my degree.

We were married, and I got pregnant on graduation night. Within the next five years, a girl and two boys were born. In order to support us, on the day our daughter was born, my husband and his mother Ella (whom I adored) opened a delicatessen/restaurant business. It was the only one of this type in our city. After five years, my in-laws retired, so they offered to transfer the business to us. At that time, I already had two very young children and a third one on the way. I was aware of the fact that the business required more than one person to operate it, so I rejected their offer and they sold their business to another person. My husband, Ben, started working for the new owner, but after a year, he realized he was not making as much money as he could have made if he owned that business. So he quit and worked several temporary jobs, and then he ended up employed by the post office as a letter carrier. He loved working at that job and continued to do so for many years.

I was a stay-at-home mom until my youngest child was in preschool. I knew that I would have to go back to work in order to pay for the education of my children. At that time, refresher courses in medical technology were not available. Since I lacked recent experience, I could not perform a job in that area. What was I supposed to do? Fortunately, my father had a good answer to this question for me. He said, "Your former job is now being done by a computer, so why don't you learn how to operate computers?"

Following his advice, I took college courses on a part-time basis, and I earned an associate degree in computer science. In this way, by studying and getting good grades, I also provided a good example for my children. And, I found employment first in the Department of Natural Resources and then at a university. Following my example, all of my children graduated from the University of Wisconsin and two of them hold advanced degrees.

My husband took early retirement from the post office and was working part time ten years before he was diagnosed with Alzheimer's. Slowly, his condition deteriorated, so he had to give up driving, and this forced him to stop working at the job he loved. He was devastated, but he found some things around the house to do. I drove him on errands and to doctors' appointments.

I continued working part time for the next ten years, paying attention to when I could receive the maximum

Social Security benefits, and I retired from the university at that optimal time.

After some time, our doctor suggested that we move from our big house to a continuing care community in order to receive help whenever we might need it. Also, we wouldn't feel isolated there because we'd make new friends. Both my husband and I were happy that we didn't need to maintain a home anymore.

With the help of our children, we managed to move to our new home—to our apartment—and, once we settled in, we developed a routine. After a few years, my husband was hospitalized with a urinary tract infection. During the recovery, he used the exercise equipment available at our Wellness Center.

Next, the doctors determined he should start using a catheter. At that time, my training in medical technology proved very helpful. I learned how to change his day bag (strapped to his leg) into the night bag (which was bigger), and then back again. We both accepted the fact that this was something that had to be done twice a day, and so our life simply evolved into a new routine. It was a different version of our time together, so I tried to joke and take it lightly.

About two years later, I noticed that my husband was not acting like he used to. I took him to the immediate care center and then back home. His discomfort worsened during the weekend, so I prepared to take him to the hospital, but he refused to go. Finally, on Monday, I took him to the emergency room, and he spent a week in the hospital, on antibiotics and under observation for his heart.

Our three children, two from out of town and the third who lives nearby, greeted him when he was released to our health center. On that Thursday, all of us visited our family doctor together, and she told us what to expect would happen to my husband if the antibiotics were withheld; essentially, this would bring a gradual peaceful death. One by one, we voted in favor of stopping the administration of antibiotics. I believe we all felt that he had lived a long, happy life, and we did not want him to reach the point at which he would not recognize us.

On Sunday, our sons took him on an outing to his favorite place—a casino. At the same time, our daughter and I explored home care agencies to find assistance that would give me some relief. On Tuesday, he came home under hospice care and the next two weeks were a blur of people coming in and out.

On Friday afternoon, the rabbi paid her weekly visit, and she asked my husband if he wanted to pray. For the first time, he said, "Yes."

As she was leaving, she said that if anything happened to him, we should send her a text, since this was the only way in which she could be reached during Shabbat. When the health care assistant prepared him for bed, he said he would probably not leave the bed. In the morning, a hospice nurse came and stayed all day. My husband passed away at 6:45 p.m., just before Shabbat was over, so the rabbi came and said a prayer for his soul.

My Prince Charming of fifty-nine years was gone! The next few days were busy with funeral arrangements, and throughout that process, I was numb and in shock. The children gave me some comfort and help, but I was not prepared for the amount of paperwork that had to be done by each of us. It helped that, before we moved to the independent living apartment, I had prepared a list of our insurance providers and of people who would someday need to be contacted for each of us.

After the paperwork was submitted and life was back on kilter, I realized I was lonely. The people from the community were acquaintances rather than good friends. I missed my husband's company, in spite of the fact that he tended to repeat himself. I was left with memories of good times and of our travels. I had the freedom to do what I wanted, no longer being tied down by the need to change the catheter bags, but I didn't really enjoy this situation. So, I started doing more for the community in which I lived.

Fortunately for me, over the years, my husband had lost any interest in financial matters. I had been paying all the bills, and I gradually controlled all our family financial activities, usually after consulting him for his approval. In order to make things easier for my children, I have prepared everything for my funeral and ordered a double monument for the cemetery. Only the date of my death needs to be added.

The current pandemic made my sense of loneliness even worse. My husband would have never understood the changes that were required in this new situation.

For me, after all these years of marriage, suddenly there was no one to talk to face-to-face—only by phone or on Zoom. My children, again, came to my rescue by checking in with me on a daily basis.

Our community director essentially had us all locked up in our apartments, and we had food delivered to our doors. We had Zoom discussions, exercising videos and movies offered on our private TV channels, and books were bought to us. No visitors were allowed to come, so our chaplain and our social worker started a Grief Support Group on Zoom.

During the summer, we could go for walks but were required to keep the proper distance from each other and to wear face coverings. Thanks to the vaccines, things began to normalize in our community, and I restored my pre-pandemic routine: breakfast, exercise class, laundry if needed, doctor appointments, meals in our restaurants, and the nightly programs—movies, opera videos, and live music entertainment—in the Grand Hall. After some time, the Grief Support Group started to meet in person. Then, one more time, the state put a new mandate to wear masks indoors, except for eating in restaurants. Exercising with a mask is not fun, so hopefully, this requirement will end soon.

As hard as it is, it is crucial to return to normal—a new normal. Being a widow has been hard, but there are others in the same boat, so friendships can and do develop. Helping and supporting one another is a priority in our community.

Sharon Rossman Hirschfeld
(widowed three years)

Sharon Hirschfeld is a wife, mother, computer analyst, and grandmother. She was married for fifty-nine and a half years before her husband died. She was a stay-at-home mom for ten years. Although she was university-educated as a medical technologist, she returned to school to study computers.

Sharon retired with twenty-six years of State Service as a computer analyst. She enjoys spending time with her two grandchildren, creating fond memories. Sharon resides in an independent living community and is active with her newfound friends, enjoying life.

.

Love in the Days of Parkinson's

Anonymous

It was a second marriage for both of us. I was almost fifty, and he (H) was sixty-three. Most of our children were in college or working, which meant that we did not have to deal with whether the children got along together, a problem that often afflicts couples who remarry. It was just the two of us, and we could do as we pleased. So we made up for all the years we had missed when living alone: traveling to faraway places, visiting family, inviting friends for dinner. H and I were happy. We were making up for the lost time watching our grandchildren grow up, appreciating our nights together just talking and reading. Our life was full and happy. The first ten years of our married life were blissful.

Except... except... there were changes that I began to notice—small details that I chose to ignore because they did not seem important. Fatigue was the first sign that something might be wrong. H needed to nap in the afternoon. When he couldn't nap, especially during the work week, he looked bedraggled at the end of the day. When we drove home at night after visiting one of our children, I took the wheel while he slept. I made excuses for his fatigue. *He's pushing seventy,*

I thought, *and he works so hard*. But then he lost his sense of smell. I asked him to see a doctor, but he refused.

"This happened to my mother also," he said. "She lost her sense of smell when she grew older. Same thing." He was a doctor, so I didn't challenge him. We attributed the change to genetics and ignored it. We both wanted so much to believe that our idyllic life would continue, so we buried our heads in the sand and pretended that all was well.

We continued to make excuses for his failing health—the lack of balance, the difficulty in swallowing—until it was clear that something serious was happening. One night, when H was driving us home, I noticed—I couldn't miss it—that he was stopping at every green light, and cars behind us were honking their frustration. I told him to pull over. I took the wheel, and he did not object. It was clear that he, too, knew that he was in trouble. I told him he could no longer drive, and, to my surprise, he agreed and I took away his keys. We also agreed that we had to see a neurologist.

I remember walking into the neurologist's office and sitting down, waiting with trepidation for the doctor to call us in.

The neurologist took one look at him and said, "You have Parkinson's disease."

"But," I blurted out, "he has no tremor."

"No matter," the doctor said. "You can tell by his face. We call it a stone face." And there it was. We couldn't pretend any longer.

One by one, our carefully constructed life began to change. We still took trips, but rather than traveling independently, we went on guided tours. Eventually, the guided tour was also too much, so we tried cruises. H could nap on the boat, I thought, while I went sightseeing with the group. Then, even a cruise was too much. Our final trip was to the Indiana Dunes, a short trip from our house. I assumed it would be an easy outing where H could stay at the resort and I could take an occasional walk to the beach. I was wrong. He could barely get out of the car and walk the few steps to the door of our cabin. So we stopped traveling. As a doctor, he knew what was in store for him: first a cane, then a walker, and finally a wheelchair.

Eventually, I hired a helper so I could have some relief from constant caregiving.

"This is no life," he would say over and over again. "You'd be better off without me."

I assured him that life with him was better than being without him even though he was sick, though if I am honest, I will have to admit that it was not always the case, and sometimes I longed to be alone with no responsibility. Taking care of him was very difficult, especially because I am not a patient person. I sighed with relief when one of the children stayed with him so I could take a trip myself.

H told me that the main causes of death in Parkinson's were falling, choking, and suicide. So I took precautions to make sure these things wouldn't happen. I pulled up the rugs and made sure his food was easy to swallow. But he had a habit of wandering at night when I was sleeping. I begged him to stay in bed at night, but I couldn't control him, and sure enough, he got up one night and tried to carry a glass of water to the bedside. First, he dropped the glass and then fell on the shards.

I was lucky that his daughter was visiting us that weekend. I called for her and she came in immediately. As I called an ambulance, she staunched the wounds, and we rode with him in the ambulance. After they stitched him up, I assumed I could bring him home by the weekend. But shortly afterward, they called me and told me he was no longer responding. I ran to the hospital where I found him lying on the bed with a ventilator. We had both agreed that neither one of us wanted to be kept alive in that manner. I knew exactly what he wanted, but even so, the decision was difficult. He looked unchanged, though he did not respond to my entreaties to wake up and talk to me.

Before he died, I spent some time with him alone and told him how much I loved him, and how much I would miss him. But, eventually, I had to leave and face the fact that, despite the ventilator, he was dead. I remembered that earlier, when we got into the ambulance, he said, "This is the end for me. Men my age who go to the hospital don't return." He had been a brilliant doctor in life and there he was, brilliant to the end, able to understand that he was dying.

My husband of twenty years was buried at Arlington Cemetery. He had always been proud of his service in the Navy during the Korean War, so it was appropriate that he be buried there. I cried during the ceremony—the sounding of Taps, the three-gun salutes, the flags—all brought tears to my eyes. The Arlington staff were solicitous and kind. I saw the niche where, someday, I will be buried next to him. The fact that I was now a widow began to dawn on me.

Finally, I said goodbye to the children and came home. At first, there was so much work to be done. H had saved everything; so we—I and the children—had to sort through reams of papers. The children took what they wanted. We donated all the medical paraphernalia to the local Goodwill Store & Donation Center. After a few days, the family left. I was alone, and for better or worse, began my new life.

My children encouraged me to move closer to them. But I did not want to be a burden on them, nor did I want to intrude on their lives. I have a life where I live, and I am too old to start anew. So I stayed where I was, where I have friends who are here to support me. Many of them have also lost a spouse.

So, I slowly forged a life without him. I take classes with adults my age. I find time to serve on two boards. I take trips to visit my sons who live in Washington, Boston, and London. I love visiting them, but coming home to an empty house is always difficult. I am always full of details about my trip that I long to tell H, but the house is quiet—no one to welcome me. To this day, there is a vacant feeling in the pit of my stomach when I return from a trip.

I miss so many things that we did together. I miss cooking for him. Now that I'm alone, a sandwich or scrambled eggs is a good enough meal for me. I miss asking him whether I should wear the white dress or the blue; asking him to read what I've written and tell me if it's OK. Are there any mistakes? Can you help me pick out my new glasses? Can you fasten my necklace? Can I borrow your handkerchief? I miss the minutia that fills married life. I cannot help asking myself—even for small problems—what would H have done? I need his opinion. I need his warmth, his kindness, his love. Talk to me, I beg. But there is no answer.

People say that when you are widowed, you should not make any quick decisions, such as moving or selling your home, and they are correct. I remembered when I was told about quick decisions after a death, and for the most part, my decisions have been calculated, and carefully thought out. That does not mean that I don't make mistakes.

In an effort to ward off loneliness, I filled my life with volunteer work, travel, theater, and concerts. It was too much. There were too many filled-in dates on my calendar. When I was young, multi-tasking was a given. I worked and raised children with little help. Now that I have turned seventy, I am no longer capable of juggling many tasks at one time. I assume that after the death of a spouse, sporadic loneliness is a given. Now I feel that it is better to stay home with a good book than to overload my life. I have lightened the load and I feel much more contented now.

I sometimes wonder what I would have done if I had known in advance that H had Parkinson's. Would I have married him? Would I have said yes to the fifteen good years, knowing that fifteen very sad years would follow? The answer is yes. I treasure the years we were together and H was healthy. I have no desire to remarry. H loved me in a way that I had never before experienced. We trusted each other; we took care of each other; we were together, physically and emotionally. It was the kind of love I had never before experienced and will never experience again.

My husband is no longer in my life, but I still talk to him. When a friend of mine recently told me I should get a face-lift, I laughed. I knew what H would say: "No unnecessary surgery."

And he was right. He was usually right, which is why I consult with him—in my mind, of course. If I can no longer be with him physically, I am with him in spirit, and in that way, he will always be with me.

The Love of My Life

Joan Galman Jones

Family is everything. If one is fortunate enough to have a loving, supportive base from where you come, it's a golden gift. I was widowed at the age of sixty-four, sixteen years ago, after forty years of marriage with, yes, the Love of My Life, Hunter.

We met as teenagers at a party in the village we lived in for our entire marriage. After an off-and-on relationship, we fell in love five years later and married. I was never more sure of any decision I made in my entire life than I was the day we were married, and to this day, I still feel that same way. He was my guy, and I was his gal.

In no time at all, we had our own children, a girl and two boys—each very special. They have the best of both me and their father. They have given me the greatest solace since Hunter died, and unconditional support, love, and consideration. I'm blessed.

Life hurried by as we bought a house, raised our family, and went to work daily. I started back to working ten years after our first child was born. I was able to be a stay-at-home mom for those formative years of our children, like many women of my generation at that time.

We had a fun and busy life and worked hard to be able to enjoy this life. Hunter was a foodie—he loved to read about it, shop for it, prepare it, and serve it to family and friends.

After our daughter's marriage and our sons' move to Colorado, we enjoyed just being the two of us again. We liked to eat and drink, do a little traveling, and just be comfortable in our home.

Shortly after this time, Hunter developed diabetes. This marked the start of a poorer health period, which included the onset of headaches and mysterious chills in his body. After a brain scan, it was discovered he had brain cancer, which resulted in surgery, chemotherapy, and radiation. This led to the heartache of cancer treatments failing to cure him. That was the very hard part—watching his decline and hoping that it would miraculously change. He died six months after being diagnosed, in our home with myself and our three adult children at his hospice bedside. I cried every day for a year and more, and still do at times.

A year after my husband's death, my elderly mother and father came to live with me at my home. They wanted to help me heal and not be alone after their son-in-law was gone. My dad lived with me for three and a half years, and my mom for ten and a half years. We did have a routine of love between us most of the time. I continued to work during this time after finding caregivers for the time I was away at work, which helped tremendously. They both died in my home—just going to sleep—with me at their bedsides.

As for my current life as a widow—but not reflecting on this description quite as much since it has been sixteen years—I am grateful to be a healthy woman with one partially replaced knee and one to go, living alone in a recent move to a lovely condo apartment after selling my home of forty-four years and living the gift of time (retirement). I love all my family relationships and close friends, and although some dear friends have died, others are here to visit and discuss the surprising turmoil of our times.

Again, my children and grandsons have been the key to my happiness as a widow. They are ever-present with texts, or phone calls and visits—it's a give-and-take that we enjoy. We all have the greatest respect and thoughtfulness for each other, including my three brothers and two sisters.

So, how do I define my widowhood? The poet Robert Frost talks of two paths diverging. Probably, but for me, Time and Love are the great healer and settler. For this, I am most thankful to God and his design for me.

Joan Galman Jones
(widowed sixteen years)

Joan and her husband, Hunter, had three children and four grandsons. After being a stay-at-home mom for ten years, she began working as a customer service rep in the insurance industry, retiring after thirty-five years.

When Joan was widowed, her parents moved into her home in an effort to keep her company, where they lived happily for the rest of their lives, her mother remaining with her until she was one-hundred-and-two.

Now retired, she has recently freshened her life, with the help of her daughter, by purging forty-four years of possessions and relocating from a vintage four-bedroom home to a two-bedroom condo with a view of her favorite park, yet still within her lifetime community of friends and family.

As the matriarch of her large family, Joan frequently hosts their gatherings, also traveling to Colorado to visit her two sons and two sisters. She occasionally overnights with her married daughter and four grandsons. Her favorite trip abroad was to Paris with her daughter and son-in-law.

The future is bright.

After the Moment Is Gone

Isabella Goldberg

Memories are a handmade quilt stitched
just for You to Burrow under
when you Shiver from moments Lost

Memories are the Building blocks of
human Essence which welded Together
Chain our souls to each other

Memories are nature's apology for the
Swift sprint of time—
an acknowledgment that

Moments are made precious
because of their Loomingly
low Supply but,

Memories are the Souvenirs
of Life which promise us
untethered contentment

Wise Actions

We All Agree

Through writing our thoughts succinctly for this anthology, we twelve have all been reminded of what makes living worthwhile—of the essential life-affirming actions to keep in mind, no matter what...

Keep Your House in Order
Advice as old as the Bible acts as a helpful forewarning for us humans.

Be Ready
If you're not yet widowed, try imagining your future possible widowhood pragmatically. Internalize the message of *Be ready*. Perhaps part of the enjoyment of marriage is relying on each other and amicably sharing the responsibilities. But self-reliance becomes necessary the minute you've lost your partner. Maintaining where you live, what you own, and what you owe takes focus and time. So does thoughtful attention to who you love, who you like, and how you treat them.

Establish Routines
If you don't have a routine, establish one—the daily structure of your existence matters to your healthy mental outlook. On a good day, waking up to familiarity counts. But on a

bad one, on the bleakest mornings of not-enough-sleep and troubling thoughts, it is imperative to just get up as usual and... brush your teeth, get some coffee, read the paper, make your bed, get dressed... and forge ahead with some chore or another to keep you active and to keep you and your home comfortably maintained. And, by the way, I'm writing this as a seventy-eight-year-old woman. So when I say, "Keep yourself maintained," that takes forethought and determination all on its own. Aging is not for sissies. Turns out, that if we don't move around every day, we simply don't feel well—we sort of stiffen up and ache. So this *routine* thing morphs right into the next category: *Life Purpose*, because why are we even living unless we're determined to enjoy it? This is not possible without personal maintenance. At this age, I live intentionally. I wish my husband had.

Understand Your Life Purpose
If you don't have a *life purpose*, get one. It's not as daunting as you might think, and could be mostly a matter of fine-tuning. Part of anyone's focus is the satisfaction of knowledge. Even reading the paper, or watching a reliable news channel, gets you learning something new. It stimulates you.

Your sorrow does not disappear. Nor the hole left by your missing mate, gone forever. For that to be filled takes a combination of books, movies, television, and time spent with those essential humans who love you and like you. Let them help you through your sadness.

Embrace Daily Laughter

Remember that life needs silliness. Find the funny and *laugh*.

A joke for the younger grandchildren:

a) Guess what...

b) What?

a) Chicken butt.

(*Butt* is obviously the key word here. Saying "butt" aloud and in front of others, especially adults, is just too much of a giggle and has to be repeated often until, eventually, you won't like me for suggesting it.)

A joke for us seasoned grown-ups:

A person spends her youth wondering about the meaning of life. Unable to find the answer through literature or further education, she finally travels to the Himalayas and climbs the highest mountain to reach what is known as the oldest and wisest of men.

Breathing heavily, she asks him, "What is the meaning of life?"

He clears his throat and replies, "Orange."

They stare at each other for many silent minutes.

Finally, she speaks. "What?" she says, "WHAT?... That's all you've got? 'THE ANSWER IS *ORANGE*'?"

The oldest of old men and wisest of all humans sighs. "Well," he says. "Isn't it?"

(There is no answer is the obvious point—so don't waste your life wondering.)

Write your joke HERE:

Stages of Grief

Elizabeth Kübler-Ross, a Swiss-American psychiatrist and author of *On Death and Dying* (Macmillan, 1969), says there are five stages of grief. Others say there are seven, but the number of stages doesn't matter as much as the validation, the understanding that there are stages, and not necessarily in this order. But certainly, we widows experience *stages* or *moods* or *phases* as we repair and adjust to our newly singular lives.

1: **Shock**, as it relates to death, is a psychological mechanism, a fog that allows us to function at a devastating time in our lives. We may not remember much of what happens during this time. This fog will protect us for days, weeks, or even months, as a protection from more serious mental problems.

2: **Denial** is an obvious escape from reality, an often unconscious defense mechanism, characterized by a refusal to accept the finality of death.

3: **Guilt**, as related to the situational "What ifs...", "What if I had...", "What if he had...", "What if she had..."

4: **Fear** of what happened, and of other matters becoming uncontrollable temporarily conquers reason.

5: **Anger** may be directed toward other family members or doctors for not preventing the death.

6:   **Despair** is often accompanied by the hopelessness of the situation, resulting in deep sadness at the loss, or of an emptiness that cannot be filled.

7:   **Acceptance** of the permanent adjustment must finally be recognized in order to move forward as the survivor.

Acknowledgments

Nancy Hunter's enthusiastic team spirit propelled me to continue this project, even as I slid into occasional languor over the complexity of it all. Establishing deadlines was energizing and kept us writers persistent. We widows sometimes ate together, cried together, read our work aloud to each other, and shared suggestions and edits, always appreciating everyone's goals toward self-improvement, and always applauding our efforts.

When I lost my drive to continue this trudge through grief, Nancy put me in touch with Gail Zelitzky, who understood and appreciated the project enough to join the team, writing a chapter and using her professional connections to further promote our shared vision.

We twelve writers wish you energizing renewals.

You're welcome. You're always welcome.

In the spirit of living life gracefully, and the fact that "We're all in this together," I'm grateful for every person in this book. The authors, the editors, the readers, their families, and mine all played roles in helping us writers develop our views comfortably.

Thank you to my authors: Celina Edelstein, Naomi Stern, Jane Hyde Hasil, Joan Galman Jones, Sharon Rossman Hirschfeld, Anonymous, Nancy Seever Hunter,

Gail Zelitzky, Kelly Judge Goldberg, Isabella Goldberg, and Nancy Wehrli Pekarek.

A very special thank you to Barbara Strassberg.

Thank you to my readers: Michael Wehrli, Sheila Wolfe, Barbara Strassberg, E. Richard Fowler, Rebecca L. Nelson, Nancy Stewart, Kelly Judge Goldberg, Michael Goldberg, Isabella Goldberg, Sharyn Wehrli Behnke, and Rebecca Handel-Fano.

It would be remiss of me if I didn't give a shout-out to my deceased husband, Bernie Judge, who famously pointed out that if it hadn't been for his craziness and our shared life, I'd have had little of interest to write about. Abundant gratitude there as well.

Suggested Reading

Ban Breathnach, Sarah. *Simple Abundance: 365 Days to a Balanced and Joyful Life*. New York, Grand Central Publishing, 1995.

Didion, Joan. *The Year of Magical Thinking*. New York, Random House, 2005.

Gawande, Atul. *Being Mortal: Medicine and What Matters in the End*. New York, Metropolitan Books, 2014.

Kubler Ross, Elizabeth. *On Death and Dying*. New York, Macmillan, 1969.

McHugh, Erin. *One Good Deed A Day*. Chronicle Books, 2012.

Sandberg, Sheryl and Adam Grant. *Option B: Facing Adversity, Building Resilience, and Finding Joy*. New York, Alfred A. Knopf, 2017.

Steines, Julie, and Virginia Freyermuth. *Norbert's Little Lessons For A Big Life*. Gallery Books, 2017.

Contributing Authors

ANONYMOUS

EDELSTEIN, CELINA, born in 1938.
She married Angelo Scanu in 1964, who was born in 1924 and died in 2018.

They had two sons from previous marriages.

GOLDBERG, ISABELLA, born in 1999.
Granddaughter of Kimbeth and Bernie Judge.

GOLDBERG, KELLY JUDGE, born 1967
Daughter of Kimbeth and Bernie Judge.

HASIL, JANE HYDE, born in 1944.
She married Jim Hasil in 1967, who was born in 1941 and died in 2019.

They had two children and five grandchildren.

HIRSCHFELD, SHARON ROSSMAN, born in 1940.
She married Benjamin Hirschfeld in 1959, who was born in 1933 and died in 2019.

They had three children and two grandchildren.

HUNTER, NANCY SEEVER, born in 1945.
She married Jack Hunter in 1977, who was born in 1944 and died in 2003.

No children.

JONES, JOAN GALMAN, born in 1942.
She married Hunter Jones in 1965, who was born in 1942 and died in 2002.

They had three children and four grandsons.

JUDGE, KIMBETH WEHRLI, born in 1944.
She married Bernie Judge in 1966, who was born in 1940 and died in 2019.

They had three children and five grandchildren.

PEKAREK, NANCY WEHRLI, born in 1942.
She married Ray Pekarek in 1963, who was born in 1942 and died in 2007.

They had four children and twelve grandchildren.

STERN, NAOMI, born in 1929.
1. She first married Fred Stern in 1950, who was born in 1929 and died in 1992.

They had four children.

2. Naomi later married Jack Jaffe in 2001, who was born in 1928 and died in 2010.

He had three adult children.

ZELITZKY, GAIL, born in 1941.
She married Al Zelitzky in 1980, who was born in 1926 and died in 2009.

She had three children; he had four, and together they had six grandchildren.

PS

My youngest adult children were less than thrilled with me somewhat-resenting their father's dark side so publicly, but I decided my candor was important, because don't tell me we don't all have difficult dark sides.

I believe it helps a person adjust to human trauma by simply pointing out the no-one's-perfect part of grief-memory. It actually soothed me missing my husband to remember purposefully the things I didn't like about him.

But as to the privacy issue, my personal view is that in this fast-paced life of never-ending decisions, I choose to focus openly on using my mistakes-in-judgment as learning tools. Lessons learned become comfortable ways to foresee future improvement. Others choose to focus on the safety of faith-based behavior, keeping their mistakes private and publicly sharing only the good. Both are valid choices. There is no judgment here.

The back story of this book is probably much more fun and interesting than this anthology of mostly careful truths. Maybe I'll write about the backstory. Maybe if I do write it, I'll choose the safety of calling it fiction.

There isn't one, but imagine an emoji here that depicts a cute little seventy-eight-year-old face smiling, almost laughing, with an important hint of sarcasm depicted in her slightly raised eyebrows.

I could call this THE END of the book, but... does anything ever *really* end?

Made in the USA
Monee, IL
01 February 2023

26806916R00079